Design Annual 1999

Design Annual 1999

Design Annual 1999

The International Annual of Design and Illustration
Das internationale Jahrbuch über Design und Illustration
Le répertoire international du design et de l'illustration

Publisher and Creative Director: B. Martin Pedersen

Editor: Heinke Jenssen
Assistant Editors: April Heck, Vivian Babuts, Laura Cramer

Art Director: Massimo Acanfora
Graphic Designers: Delfin Chavez, Carol Ford
Photographer: Alfredo Parraga

Published by Graphis Inc.

(opposite) Nike, Inc. *(following page)* Cathleen Toelke *(page 6)* The Attik Design

Contents Inhalt Sommaire

Remarks: We extend our heartfelt thanks to contributors throughout the world who have made it possible to publish a wide and international spectrum of the best work in the field of design. Entry instructions for all Graphis Books may be requested from: **Graphis Inc.**, 141 Lexington Avenue, New York, NY 10016-8193 or visit our Web site, www.graphis.com

Anmerkungen: Unser Dank gilt den Einsendern aus aller Welt, die es uns durch ihre Beiträge ermöglicht haben, ein breites, internationales Specktrum der besten Arbeiten zu veröffentlichen. Teilnahmebedingungen für die Graphis-Bücher sind erhältlich bei: **Graphis Inc.**, 141 Lexington Avenue, New York, NY 10016-8193. Besuchen Sie uns im World Wide Web, www.graphis.com

Remerciements: Nous remercions les participants du monde entier qui ont rendu possible la publication de cet ouvrage offrant un panorama complet des meilleurs travaux. Les modalités d'inscription peuvent être obtenues auprès de: **Graphis Inc.**, 141 Lexington Avenue, New York, NY 10016-8193. Rendez-nous visite sur notre site web: www.graphis.com

ISBN: 1-888001-48-8 © Copyright under universal copyright convention copyright © 1998 by Graphis Inc., New York, NY 10016. Jacket and book design copyright © 1998 by Pedersen Design, 141 Lexington Avenue, New York, NY 10016, USA. No part of this book may be reproduced in any form without written permission of the publisher. Printed by DNP.

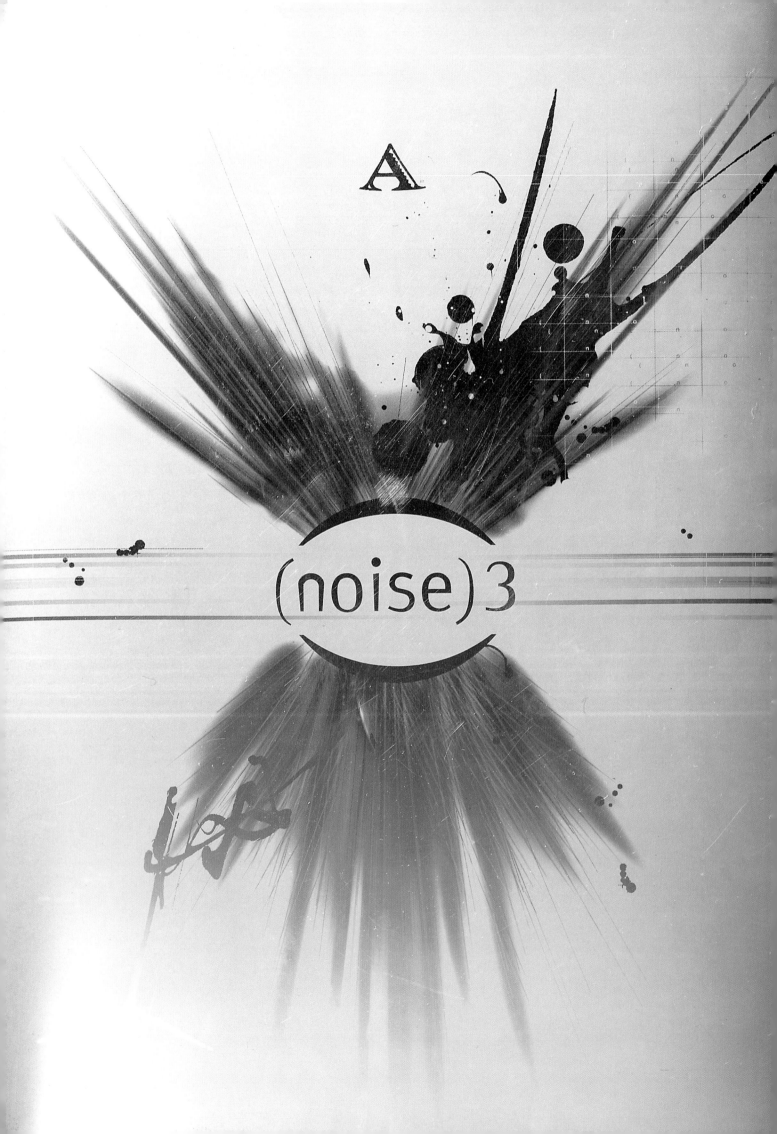

Commentary **Kommentar** Commentaire

Lewis Blackwell: Of Water Babies, Swooshes, Teletubbies, and You

I was going to introduce this commentary with the grand title of "The Difficulty of Being Good in a World of Choice." Then I had another thought—shouldn't it be "a world of doubt?" Choice and doubt—two sides of the same coin. Somehow we want to remove doubt and make the right choice. And, every day, that is part of the job of the designer—to get it right, to make it good. Most of us would like to be good most of the time. Something in our upbringing, or our sense of self-preservation, or perhaps even some consciously worked-out and chosen values, tells us that being good is good for us. At its simplest, the reasoning is that of Mrs. Doasyouwouldbedoneby, the moralistic character who appears in the nineteenth century English novel THE WATER BABIES *by Charles Kingsley. In those times, a stern morality,*

rooted in the order of religion and state, was ready to slap down any stray thoughts. Now we have to make and re-make our values, a question-and-answer process that hungers for new juxtapositions. In a century that has given us Cubism, collage, jazz and the potential for total annihilation of the species and much more, we have arrived at a point of constant interrogation about space, time and meaning.

In design, we do have creative awards to tell us what is good this year—judgements based on an often mysterious mix of innovation, craft, excellence and other shared standards. We have effectiveness awards to tell us that good can be measured as sales or by other quantifiable means. But once it did not seem so relative: "good design" was there to be aimed at like a bullseye. After the Second World War, for example, the Good Design award and exhibition program was established in the U.S., while in the U.K. the Design Council also espoused a puritanical agenda of goodness. Other nations set up similar schemes, full of ideals and hope (although, admittedly, they were often motivated in part by a need to kick-start consumerism post-war). Underpinned by the mass religion of Modernism, these bodies could publish their propaganda with little fear of challenge. They set the agenda and yet also remained the establishment.

Now, we don't have a vision of how things should be—instead we have, at best, choices. And we always question them, rather than have the confidence to believe in any one as the answer. Whether designers or consumers, we embrace diversity. Just look at the shopping malls, the multi-channel televisions, the range of clothing styles, the dazzling array of forms and colors of cars.

Intriguingly, both the aforementioned Good Design program and the Design Council have been reborn or relaunched in recent years—seemingly unaware that their optimism is actually rooted in a model of society and production that does not operate any more, at least not in the (so-called) developed countries. That is, in a world that now contains aggressive global media, post-industrial western nations, third world countries

holding superpowers to ransom, and more, the role of design in solving our society's ills is confused. Good easily turns bad. And even more often, good seems hard to find in the first place.

Consider: Nike trainers and other products, along with their graphics, were on a 20-year roll of being fêted by the sporting cognoscenti, awards juries and fashionable slices of youth culture. They were a beacon of goodness, from the waffle sole to the poetic billboards and commercials. More recently there has been some less flattering coverage of Nike's business. Suddenly it didn't seem so cool to admire the wonderful waffle or the powerful swoosh logo. So have my shoes become less well-designed? Should I scorn the swoosh, that simple but so recognizable symbol?

Another example of complexity: "Teletubbies" is a hugely successful internationally award-winning children's TV series, featuring four colorful characters who gambol around munching tubby toast in an other-worldly park. They have spawned a multi-million dollar industry of merchandising. My daughter will insist on wearing her costume for breakfast. Is this yellow floppy-hooded outfit a thing of genius, of beauty, a brilliant piece of characterization and identity? My daughter might say "yes" and who am I to argue? And yet the design works on many levels, touching both emotion and reason, offering both originality and functionality (it is warm and washable).

Choices. Now, good and bad arrives in one definition. Opposites are just two ways of seeing the same thing, it is sometimes said. And, indeed, from my experience judging design awards I know that debate often centers around work that part of the jury finds excellent, and another roundly condemns. All too often, this results in stalemate—so nobody's first choice actually appears (Note: this is not how Graphis operates!).

But I would like to end on a plea: there is a solution to the problem of choice in this relativist, somewhat value-less world. Show true commitment. Don't compromise, and don't fail to apply your skills to what you really care about. Enjoy this book, but then get back to your own values. Accept no imitations.

Lewis Blackwell lives in London, working as a writer and editor. He is editor and publisher of CREATIVE REVIEW *magazine and the author of several best-selling design books including* THE END OF PRINT: THE GRAPHIC DESIGN OF DAVID CARSON, *and (with Neville Brody)* G1. *His most recent books are* REMIX: 20TH CENTURY TYPE *and forthcoming, with Laurie and Scott Makela,* WHEREISHERE. *Pictured opposite: Lewis Blackwell and daughter, photo courtesy Lewis Blackwell.*

Pentagram Design: "Bring in 'Da Noise, Bring in 'Da Funk"

What would a New York City street look like if it could shout? It might look a lot like the posters and billboards for BRING IN 'DA NOISE, BRING IN 'DA FUNK, *the Public Theater's Tony-award-winning theatrical production. The show's explosive promotional campaign, launched in 1996 and still going strong, hasn't missed a beat, keeping in step as the play made the leap uptown to Broadway, and even as the show experienced changes in its starring line-up. Winner of a multitude of awards, including Advertising Age's 1996 Images of the Year award, the campaign's lush visibility has brought critical attention and a new wave of talent and fans to the Public Theater, and skyrocketing ticket sales have generated significant extra income for the non-profit organization. Impressed with the relentless energy of the graphically-arresting campaign, Graphis took a moment to talk to some of its key choreographers.*

Evan Shapiro, *Marketing Director, Fourfront Press & Marketing, revealed the necessity of being adaptable to change—a survival tactic that clearly has kept the campaign alive and kicking over time.*

"When producer George Wolfe first described the potential theatrical production to designer Paula Scher and myself, he charged us with the task of changing the landscape for marketing musical theater, just as he was embarking on a journey which would forever change the landscape of creating musical theater itself.

"The ability to adapt the design to both the direction of George's vision, and to the challenge of the varying media, has been a major force behind the show's ever-changing marketing approach in the New York and national marketplace. In many ways, Paula and Pentagram Design have set the standard for the integration of design, marketing and message. The continuing success of this show is a testament to the fact that her efforts have succeeded in redefining how we look at furthering the mission and message of quality artistic endeavors."

Rick Elice, *Creative Director, Serino Coyne Inc. advertising agency, spoke to Graphis about some of the economic and demographic challenges that the design team overcame.*

"Broadway budgets are miniscule by Madison Avenue standards. *Noise/Funk* began off-Broadway at a non-profit theater—we're talking a budget that was practically non-existent! We needed impact quickly and affordably. Paula Scher devised a thrillingly contemporary initial solution to that challenge with the help of photographer Richard Avedon. Movement and texture didn't grow simply from the posters' photographic image, Paula made the words soar, scream and blast.

"When George Wolfe announced his intention to bring the show uptown to Broadway, it was not a case of simply packing up and changing theaters. On opening night at the Ambassador Theater, traditional Broadway became a new, young, energized, intelligent, poetic Broadway. But exciting as it was, we had to face commercial reality. We had to demonstrate to the conventional Broadway audience that *Noise/Funk* wasn't noisy, funky or scary."

Paula Scher, *Designer, Pentagram Design, is the campaign's art director. With senior designer Anke Stohlmann, Scher continues to create compelling designs whose power extends beyond the theatre marquees and onto the very streets and sidewalks of New York.*

"I've had a long relationship with the Public Theater, starting with the redesign of the theater's brand identity. It's always a challenge to continue reinventing their image, to stand outside of their whole history and try to keep an objective eye—and to always keep the conversation alive between the theater and the city.

"We've certainly met our share of challenges. One of the exciting things about the *Noise/Funk* campaign was designing for the whole city of New York. What would make it synonymous with the grit and romance of a great city? The poster's improvisational scheme—bright colors and silhouetted photos, combined with street style—contributed dramatically to our vision. To our delight, the images and vocabulary captured the attention of New Yorkers and tourists alike, and has become a real part of the city's iconography and visual landscape.

"In preparation for the departure of the show's star, Savion Glover, our task was to subtly transform the poster campaign in an exciting way, yet still carry the power of Richard Avedon's original famous shot of Savion. We chose the image of the tap-dancing foot in place of the portrait. Six months later, Lois Greenfield's fabulous pictures of the remaining cast members were incorporated into the design. In this way we successfully played down the fact that the star had departed, without compromising any of the strength of the campaign."

George C. Wolfe *is producer of the Public Theatre, and Producer, Director, and Co-conceiver of "Bring in 'Da Noise, Bring in 'Da Funk."*

"Most posters for Broadway musicals are stuck in time, circa 1966. *Noise/Funk*, the show, is both highly theatrical and has a 1990's in-your-face kind of energy. In talking with Paula, we wanted to create a poster that possessed the same dynamic. Consequently, everything—from our original teaser campaign to changing the individual image of the show every five months—is intended to keep the look of *Noise/Funk* fresh and perpetually in the moment."

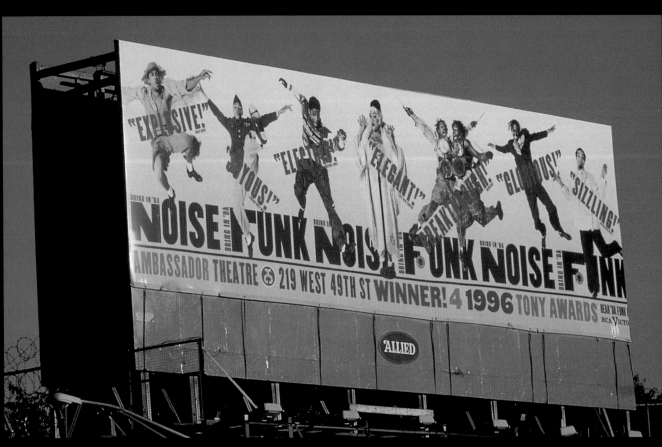

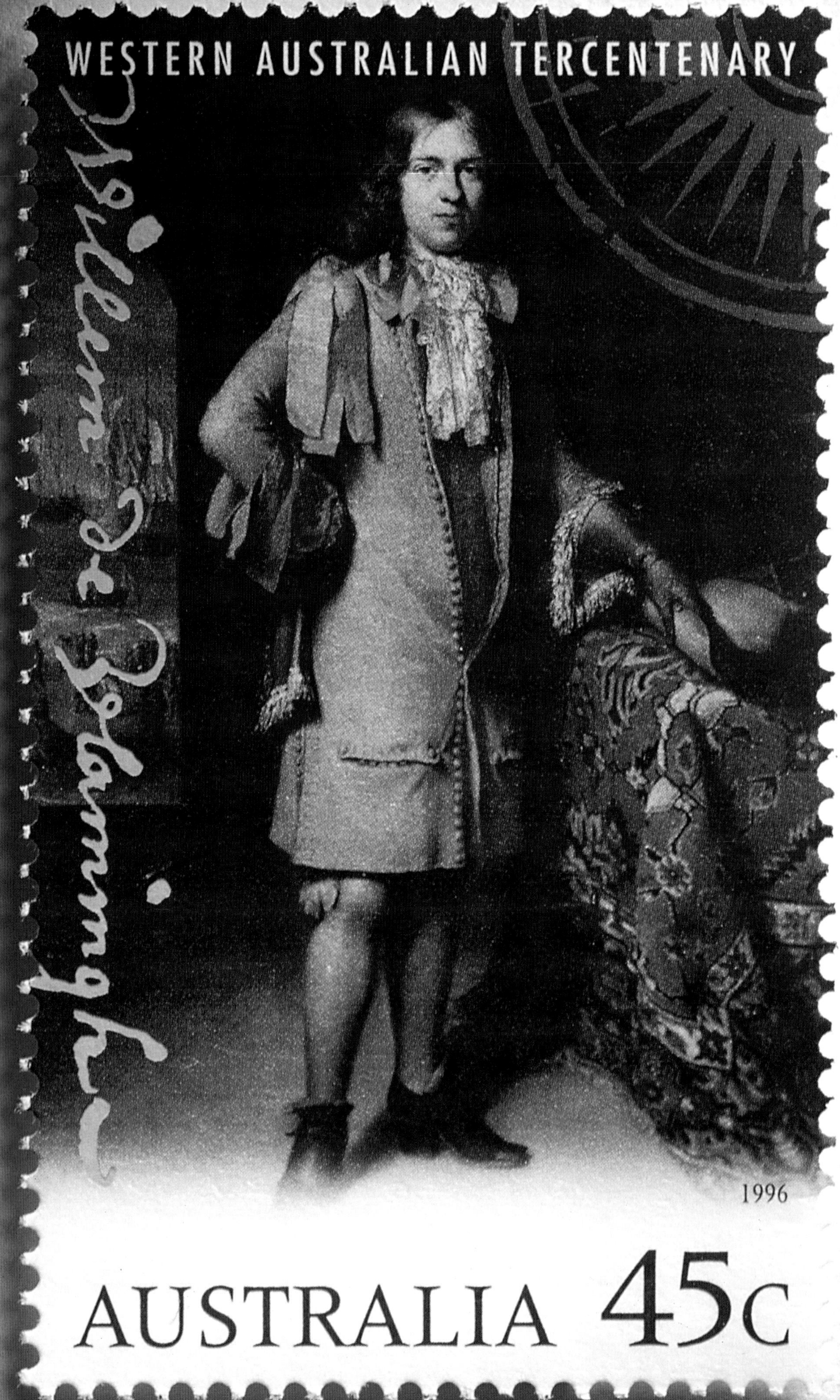
WESTERN AUSTRALIAN TERCENTENARY
1996
AUSTRALIA 45c

When sorting through various stamps for this Design Annual, we at Graphis were imme-diately delighted by a particular funny-looking fellow on an appealing and colorful Aus-tralian stamp. Our initial delight subsided into intrigue, however, as we thought about the actual logistics of a stamp commission for a design company. And so, we contacted the cre-ative source, our down-under neighbors at Asprey Di Donato Design of Victoria, Aus-tralia, and received the following behind-the-scenes glimpse into the making of the stamp from one of the firm's directors, Peter Asprey: "The stamp for Australia Post was issued on November 1, 1996, and celebrates the 300th anniversary of the Dutchman Willem De Vlamingh's sea voyage. This 1696 journey was the last large-scale voyage undertaken

by the Dutch East India Company, during which De Vlam-ingh mapped a large part of the Australian coast.

"This job was notable for its lack of reference material. The research department of the Australia Post provided us with everything they could find—two books from their own research library, both about nautical explorations. As De Vlamingh's voyage was relatively unspectacular in terms of discovery, both books touched only briefly on his trip.

"Our initial designs attempted to include many elements, most importantly the only known portrait of Willem De Vlamingh, for which Australia Post provided a transparency, along with one of a historical map tracing his route. We were initially asked to design a pair of stamps with one con-tinuous image running across them both. This allowed us to experiment with blending the portrait with illustrations of his ship route and an engraving of the ships landing. We also tried layering De Vlamingh's handwriting (from an entry in his log) over the image. [See images, this page]. The Committee later decided that a single stamp design was required, so we were unable to continue in this direction. We changed the orientation of the stamp, simplified the graphic content, and gained permission to slightly crop the portrait for practical reasons. We realized that despite its lim-ited nature, the historical material would tell the story, so we minimized the graphic elements and used only a subtle con-trast between the explorer's signature script and a contem-porary sans serif font.

"The standard of stamp design in Australia is very high so we were conscious with this job to try not to be too clever. In the late 1960's, Australia Post made a deliberate effort to modernize stamp design in Australia. By employing the tal-ents of then up-and-coming designers and illustrators like Brian Sadgrove and Alex Stitt, Australia Post built a reputa-tion for vision and innovation in their work. These days, this reputation ensures that stamp remains well-respected within the design community.

"The cultural significance of this type of work adds a whole new dimension to our role as designers. We get a great deal of satisfaction from designing stamps—it feels like we are con-tributing as well as selling to the public.

"The resulting design was approved by the Stamp Advisory Committee, and Australia Post was happy with the final out-come. At least, we think they were happy, because our rela-tionship with them has continued since, and, in fact, we are working on our second pre-stamped envelope for Australia Post as we speak."

ART&IDEAS

PHAIDON

Many of us have a distant memory of lugging an art history book across campus to class—that weighty, encyclopedia-like chunk of a book that may have served just as well for a doorstop. Dig a little farther into those mental archives, and you may recall a dog-eared index, scribbling notes in the narrow margins, sketching paintings for a set of flashcards you wouldn't dare reveal to anyone—especially not that sweetheart who sat in the second row of your art class. Where were the Art & Ideas series when you needed them? Well, they're finally here, and in a very big way: in the spring of 1997, Phaidon Press (UK) launched their Art & Ideas series of art books to an exceptionally enthusiastic reception. "The most likely pretender to the World of Art crown," England's own Royal Academy magazine has dubbed the Phaidon newcomer, referring to the classic Thames and Hudson's series.

Under the art direction of Phaidon's Alan Fletcher, the grand-scale project (aimed to eventually number 100+ editions) wasn't all smooth sailing from the start. The plan, simply put: to create a distinctive style for a series of inexpensive pocket books on the entire history of art and artists. The design team came up with a format that would allow for easy reading, presenting just enough text per page to absorb in one quick read. The format would also mesh picture and text together to avoid having to flip though pages to find references—which would also mean taking great pains to design and redesign each page. Indeed, each book would become the responsibility of one designer, because, although the grid was fixed, designed on a central and vertical axis, the layout would depend on the subject and materials.

"When the design style was first presented," says Fletcher, "it was unenthusiastically received by the editors. They felt the larger type and spacing looked childlike, the inevitable extra thickness of the book unwieldy, the grey type difficult to read. However," Fletcher continues, "the publisher was convinced, and the subsequent success of the series has proved him right." (The editors have definitely warmed to the design since.) In a real turn of the tables in fact, one of the series' designers, Phil Barnes, claims "the publisher is actually more interested with the look and flow of the design than us! We [the designers] are probably more interested in the relationship of the text and image."

At any rate, Phaidon Press took a gamble, and it paid off. But why the whole of art history—why now? Another of the series' designers, Quentin Newark of Atelier Works (his firm also conceived the series' cover style) answers, "The world of art publishing has long looked with envy at the 'World of Art' series. In 40 years, it has sold about 25 million copies, so to compete with success like this was like starting a marathon when the leader is 20 miles ahead...."

"The way to triumph in the long run," Newark goes on to say, "was through every detail being just right; by doing everything better than 'World of Art': the choice of images, their size and frequency, the graphic style and consistency, print and paper quality." As for the noticeably crisp covers, Atelier Works "exercised restraint," says Newark, "putting the title in tiny text size in a sea of white, and choosing just one piece of art to sum up a whole life's work, or 1000 years of history. Since most books in a bookstore are sitting on a shelf, spine out, the icon is repeated on the spine, making a tiny, beautiful frieze."

"The artists' work," he says, "is the point, not the designers'."

Morla Design: Levi Strauss

Morla Design has a lot of tricks up their sleeve—a multi-faceted company, they offer creative services encompassing print collateral, logo design, book design, corporate identity, packaging, signage, and on-screen graphics and animation. But perhaps the best magic has happened in their 18-year collaboration with Levi Strauss & Co., during which Morla Design has had their hands on everything from branding, point-of-purchase materials, posters, retail shop design, and interactive displays. You won't need to look far to find the evidence: for one, they designed the 3200 square foot

in-store shop seen at Macy's Herald in New York City. They also designed a series of posters in the 1980's [see opposite] which took a radical departure from the full-color, western imagery previously used to advertise Levi's 501 jeans. The posters were targeted at the 14–24-year-old audience, and were instrumental in Levi Strauss & Co's campaign to introduce the 501 jean to the east coast. Still produced today, in fact, the posters are in their eight millionth printing. More recently, they have created a portfolio of five poster portraits, depicting international and abstract images designed to communicate metaphorical allusions to Levi's jeans. The individuality of the poster is further emphasized by using five internationally-known photographers and illustrators, including Amy Guip, Jock McDonald, Matthew Rolston, Amy Butler and Leigh Wells. The series revives the tradition of Levi's "non-specific" product posters. Graphis spoke with Jennifer Morla about her work with Levi Strauss: "A fundamental aspect of our design concept," she says, "is the ability to create branding identities which translate smoothly to and from a variety of mediums. And because of our extensive knowledge of their product line, retail environment, and target consumer base, we often called when a marketing challenge is at the point of being identified." She also talked about a particularly eye-catching project, the Levi's Youthwear shop, a 1300 square-foot

in-store shop designed as a futuristic laboratory for kids [pictured above]. "We knew that the design must accomplish two key tasks." she explains. "First, facilitate easy shopping for parents, and second, get kids to enjoy trying on the product, thereby making their shopping experience fun and memorable. We created a very tactile environment: a completely mirrored, interactive dressing room where the kids can see digitized images of themselves on video and experience the jeans while dancing to strobe lights and custom channel audio. Silkscreened copy appears on mirrored surfaces in fun, futuristic 'lab-speak.' An interactive kiosk entertains and educates while parents shop." (It certainly makes a trip to grocery store pale by comparison.)

And one needn't search far for evidence of Morla Design's success. Word on the street—worldwide in fact—is that Levi's are the most wanted jeans around; even used pairs are going for more than their original price these days. The brand could be called the Nike of jeans—a product so at one with its masterfully-designed aura and image, the little red Levi's tab is at least as coveted by consumers as the infamous swoosh. And it's a brand that communicates much more than an all-American, kid-next-door sensibility. The brand speaks to a global audience whose tastes and demographics vary vastly, and yet are united by something they love: Levi's.

Design Annual 1999

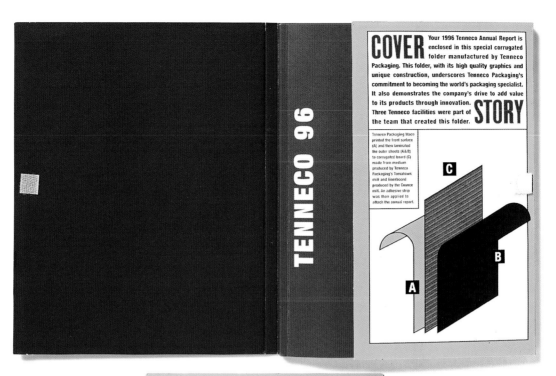

COVER Your 1996 Tenneco Annual Report is enclosed in this special corrugated folder manufactured by Tenneco Packaging. This folder, with its high quality graphics and unique construction, underscores Tenneco Packaging's commitment to becoming the world's packaging specialist. It also demonstrates the company's drive to add value to its products through innovation. Three Tenneco facilities were part of the team that created this folder. **STORY**

Tenneco Packaging Waco printed the front surface (A) and then laminated the outer sheets (A&B) to corrugated board (C) made from medium produced by Tenneco Packaging's Tomahawk mill and linerboard produced by the Counce mill. An adhesive strip was then applied to attach the annual report.

TENNECO 96

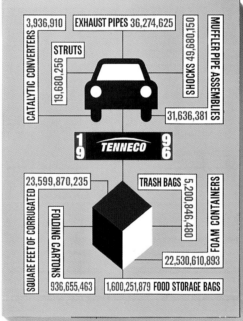

CATALYTIC CONVERTERS 3,936,910

EXHAUST PIPES 36,274,625

STRUTS 19,680,256

MUFFLER PIPE ASSEMBLIES

SHOCKS 96,580,150

31,636,381

19 TENNECO **96**

SQUARE FEET OF CORRUGATED 23,599,870,235

TRASH BAGS 5,200,846,480

FOAM CONTAINERS

FOLDING CARTONS 936,655,463

22,530,610,893

1,600,251,879 FOOD STORAGE BAGS

Design Firm: Pentagram Design
Art Director: Lowell Williams
Designers: Bill Carson, Lowell Williams
Photographer: Arthur Meyerson
Copywriter: Mary Wiggins
Client: Tenneco

THE NEW TENNECO. When Tenneco shareowners voted on December 10, 1996, to spin off the new Tenneco and Newport News Shipbuilding as independent companies and merge Tenneco Energy with El Paso Energy, the last step in a restructuring program that began five years ago was completed, and a new chapter in Tenneco's corporate history began. We are now an automotive parts and packaging company with revenues of roughly $6.6 billion. What, you may be asking, do Tenneco Automotive and Tenneco Packaging have in common? Both are large global manufacturers. Both have a high potential for growth, particularly in markets outside the United States. Both should profit from changing demographics and economic trends. Both offer a great opportunity to benefit from our management processes. And most importantly, both have the capability to create more value for you, our shareowner. We are a more focused company, and although we have reduced Tenneco's size and scope, we intend to grow. We intend to grow revenues twofold and operating income at an even faster rate by the year 2001,

FORMED THE NEW TENNECO

9 **46**

- with two businesses, Tenneco Automotive and Tenneco Packaging and the shared services unit, Tenneco Business Services
- Completed sale of Case Corporation, raising $816 million from final offering
- Made six key acquisitions and formed two joint ventures
- Announced and completed the spin-off of Newport News Shipbuilding
- Announced and completed the merger of Tenneco Energy with El Paso Energy
- Headquarters moved to Greenwich, Connecticut

NAMED ONE OF THE 100 BEST managed companies in the world by *Industry Week* magazine

pled us five flexibility to the level of that, here's ales. In the revenues to adership in stems. More omakers are our packag- ciently mar- er customer g ourselves product cat- responsible emblies. On out Tenneco o manufac- eo's future. s that form ing forward.

Heavy-duty trucks like this Freightliner class 8 tractor routinely cover 100,000 miles of road annually. That kind of mileage translates to a solid market for heavy-duty exhaust components. Tenneco Automotive expanded its capabilities in this important replacement market with the acquisition of the heavy-duty exhaust business of Stemco in November.

22

23

Tenneco Inc. and Consolidated Subsidiaries Statements of Income

(Millions Except Share Amounts)	1996	1995	1994
	Years Ended December 31,		
Revenues			
Net sales and operating revenues —			
Automotive	$ 2,980	$ 2,479	$ 1,989
Packaging	3,602	2,752	2,184
Intergroup sales and other	(10)	(10)	(7)
	6,572	5,221	4,166
Other income, net	76	39	(2)
	6,648	5,260	4,164
Costs and Expenses			
Cost of sales (exclusive of depreciation shown below)	4,762	3,737	3,050
Engineering, research and development	82	67	43
Selling, general and administrative	657	588	473
Depreciation, depletion and amortization	309	196	142
	6,020	4,588	3,708
Income before interest expense, income taxes and minority interest	628	672	456
Interest expense (net of interest capitalized)	195	160	104
Income tax expense	194	231	114
Minority interest	21	23	—
Income from continuing operations	218	258	238
Income from discontinued operations, net of income tax	428	477	214
Income before extraordinary loss	646	735	452
Extraordinary loss, net of income tax	(236)	—	(5)
Income before cumulative effect of change in accounting principle	410	735	447
Cumulative effect of change in accounting principle, net of income tax	—	—	(39)
Net income	410	735	408
Preferred stock dividends	12	12	12
Net income to common stock	$ 398	$ 723	$ 396
Per Share			
Average number of shares of common stock outstanding	170,635,277	173,995,941	180,064,006
Earnings (loss) per average share of common stock —			
Continuing operations	$ 1.28	$ 1.48	$ 1.32
Discontinued operations	2.43	2.68	1.13
Extraordinary loss	(1.38)	—	(.03)
Cumulative effect of change of accounting principle	—	—	(.22)
	$ 2.33	$ 4.16	$ 2.20
Cash dividends per share of common stock	$ 1.80	$ 1.60	$ 1.60

The accompanying notes to financial statements are an integral part of these statements of income.

58

Tenneco Inc. and Consolidated Subsidiaries Balance Sheets

(Millions)	1996	1995
	December 31,	
Assets		
Current assets:		
Cash and temporary cash investments	$ 62	$ 354
Receivables —		
Customer notes and accounts, net	561	351
Affiliated companies	—	117
Income taxes	—	41
Other	138	54
Inventories	878	838
Deferred income taxes	95	23
Prepayments and other	189	168
	1,923	1,946
Other assets:		
Long-term notes receivable	20	16
Goodwill and intangibles, net	1,341	1,024
Deferred income taxes	60	52
Pension assets	547	433
Other	444	239
	2,412	1,764
Plant, property and equipment, at cost	4,670	4,138
Less—Reserves for depreciation, depletion and amortization	1,618	1,450
	3,252	2,656
Net assets of discontinued operations	—	1,045
	$7,587	$7,413
Liabilities and Shareowners' Equity		
Current liabilities:		
Short-term debt (including current maturities on long-term debt)	$ 239	$ 384
Payables —		
Trade	651	589
Affiliated companies	—	47
Taxes accrued	91	45
Accrued liabilities	308	237
Other	335	257
	1,621	1,559
Long-term debt	2,067	1,648
Deferred income taxes	476	435
Postretirement benefits	168	156
Deferred credits and other liabilities	305	166
Commitments and contingencies		
Minority interest	304	301
Shareowners' equity:		
Common stock	2	957
Stock Employee Compensation Trust (common stock held in trust)	—	(215)
Premium on common stock and other capital surplus	2,642	3,602
Cumulative translation adjustments	23	26
Retained earnings (accumulated deficit)	(21)	(469)
	2,646	3,901
Less - Shares held as treasury stock, at cost	—	753
	2,646	3,148
	$7,587	$7,413

The accompanying notes to financial statements are an integral part of these balance sheets.

59

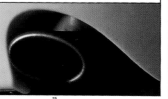

GLOBAL EXPANSION. As the major automakers become more global, we are committed to growing along with them. We supply virtually every vehicle manufacturer in the world – and we do that from 67 facilities located in 21 countries serving customers in over 100 countries. Although North America, Western Europe, and Japan will continue to dominate original equipment markets, we are also investing in markets through acquisitions and joint ventures in places like Eastern Europe, South America, India, and China. We believe the potential growth in these markets is significant. As vehicle manufacturers become established and these new cars age, aftermarket demand will follow, and we should continue to leverage the strength of our Monroe and Walker premium brands.

You'll find our exhaust systems on everything from a high-volume, lower-cost Volkswagen to the highly engineered Porsche Carrera. In fact, Tenneco Automotive's Walker exhaust system is on every Carrera built in the world today.

25

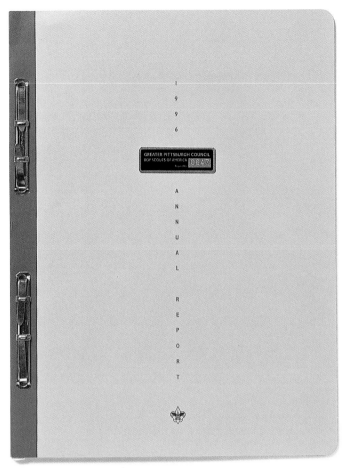

1
9
9
6

A
N
N
U
A
L

R
E
P
O
R
T

GREATER PITTSBURGH COUNCIL
BOY SCOUTS OF AMERICA 0647

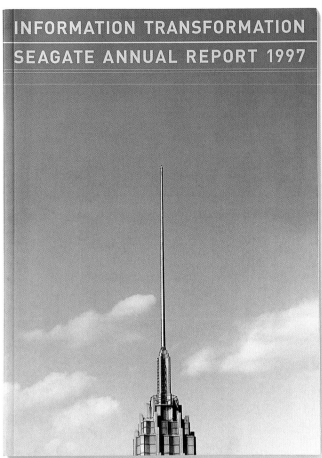

INFORMATION TRANSFORMATION
SEAGATE ANNUAL REPORT 1997

EQUAL
ACCESS
TO THE LAW
SHOULD NOT CARRY
A PRICE TAG

CHICAGO VOLUNTEER LEGAL SERVICES
1997 ANNUAL REPORT

Executive Risk

NO
SPEED
LIMIT

1996 Annual Report

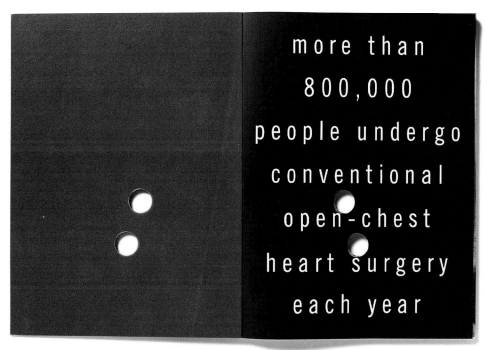

more than
800,000
people undergo
conventional
open-chest
heart surgery
each year

(opposite top left)
Design Firm: John Brady
Design Consultants
Art Director: John Brady
Designer: Jim Bolander
Copywriter: Amy Franz
Client: Greater Pittsburgh Council
Boy Scouts of America

(top right)
Design Firm: EAI
Creative Director: Phil Hamlett
Designer: Todd Simmons
Photographer: Andrew Bordwin
Copywriter: Wilson da Silva
Client: Seagate Technology

(bottom left)
Design Firm: Froeter Design Co.
Art Director, Designer: Tim Bruce
Photographer: Tony Armour
Copywriters: Lee M. Witte,
Margaret C. Benson
Client: Chicago Volunteer Legal
Services

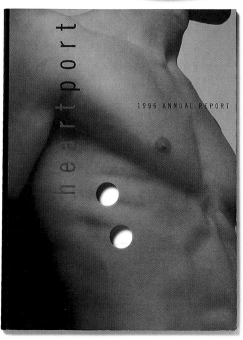

(bottom right)
Design Firm: Ted Bertz Graphic Design
Creative Director, Art Director: Ted Bertz
Designers: Ted Bertz, Mimi LaPoint
Photographer: Paul Horton, Jim Coon
Copywriter: Tim Curry
Client: Executive Risk Inc.

(this page)
Design Firm: Cahan & Associates
Creative Director, Art Director: Bill Cahan
Designer: Craig Bailey
Photographers: Ken Schles,
Tony Stromberg, William McLeod
Copywriter: Jim Weiss
Client: Heartport, Inc.

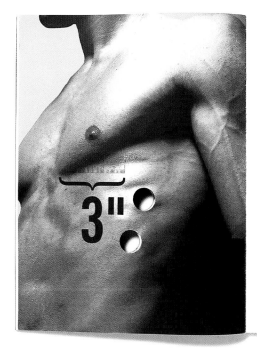

Port-Access™
Systems enable
surgeons to
perform a wide
range of heart
operations
through small
incisions
between the ribs

OPERATING REVENUE PER AVAILABLE SEAT MILE
Scheduled Service Only

OPERATING EXPENSE PER AVAILABLE SEAT MILE
Scheduled Service Only

S tick to what you're good at.

Since Southwest's inception, we have fundamentally adhered to our shorthaul, high frequency, low-fare, point-to-point market niche. ♥ As a consequence, Southwest provides service only to communities that have ample local traffic to profitably support our high-frequency operation.

Since our focus is on local, not connecting, shorthaul traffic, we do not interline with other jet carriers or have any commuter feeder relationships. As a consequence, approximately 80 percent of our Customers fly nonstop.

Southwest schedules its aircraft on a point-to-point as opposed to a hub-and-spoke basis. Our extensive point-to-point routing system provides more direct nonstop routings to better serve the needs of the business as well as the leisure shorthaul passenger. By avoiding hubs, we minimize connections, delays, and our Customers' total travel time. In addition, many of the airports we serve are conveniently located satellite or downtown airports such as Dallas Love Field, Houston Hobby, Chicago Midway, Oakland, Burbank, Ft. Lauderdale, and Baltimore. These airports are typically less congested than hub airports and, therefore, improve our ability to maintain our outstanding ontime performance record.

Although we served only 46 airports at the end of 1995, we had over 2,000 flights per day. The average number of daily departures per airport was approximately 45. Our largest airports are Phoenix Sky Harbor, Dallas Love Field, Houston Hobby, and Las Vegas McCarran with 168, 137, 136, and 128 daily flights, respectively. At the airports

we serve, we consistently have among the largest number of Customers boarded of all airlines. We ranked first or second in terms of Customers boarded in the majority of our 46 airports served in 1995.

As a result of the combination of low fares, high frequencies, convenience, and outstanding Customer Service, we dominate the majority of the shorthaul markets we serve. We consistently rank first in market share in approximately 80 to 90 percent of our top 100 city-pair markets and, in the aggregate, hold 60 to 70 percent of the total market share. Southwest also carries the most passengers in the top 100 U.S. markets despite serving only 41 of them.

"Our focus is, and always has been, shorthaul, point-to-point travel. That's why 80 percent of our Customers fly nonstop."

— GARY C. KELLY
Vice President-Finance, Chief Financial Officer

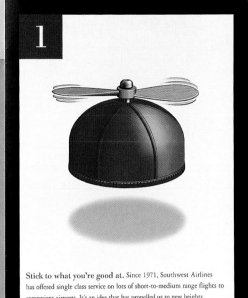

1

Stick to what you're good at. Since 1971, Southwest Airlines has offered single class service on lots of short-to-medium range flights to convenient airports. It's an idea that has propelled us to new heights.

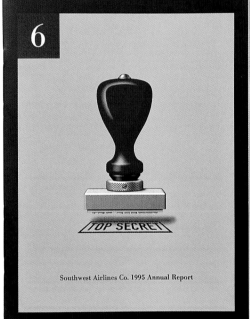

6

Southwest Airlines Co. 1995 Annual Report

Design Firm: Sibley/Peteet Design
Art Directors: Tim McClure, Rex Peteet
Designers: Rex Peteet, Matt Heck, K. C. Teis
Illustrator: Peter Kramer
Client: Southwest Airlines

PASSENGERS CARRIED PER EMPLOYEE
Scheduled Service Only

PASSENGER REVENUE PER PASSENGER MILE
Scheduled Service Only

K eep it simple.

Simplicity is a basic philosophy at Southwest Airlines. ♥ Southwest was built to meet the needs of the shorthaul, point-to-point traveler, and this is our focus. We fly only one aircraft type, the Boeing 737. This drastically simplifies scheduling, maintenance, flight operations, and training activities.

At yearend 1995, we had 224 Boeing 737 aircraft in our fleet, consisting of 149 -300s; 50 -200s; and 25 -500s. In 1994, Southwest agreed to be the launch customer with the Boeing Company for the third time and will add the new -700 model to our fleet beginning in fourth quarter 1997. Our agreement with Boeing allows for a comparatively lower capital cost, and the -700 is expected to be quieter, more fuel-efficient and more easily maintainable than its -300 counterpart. The new aircraft model should also have the capability to fly faster, longer, and higher. The -700 is expected to carry the same type rating as the rest of the 737 family, thereby allowing for the same simplified scheduling, training, and maintenance as today. Operating a single aircraft type has proven to be efficient and safe for our high frequency, shorthaul, point-to-point market focus.

From an operational perspective, we utilize simple, quick, and efficient ticketing and boarding procedures to minimize Customers' total trip time. We also avoid costly and complicated interlining arrangements with other carriers.

Since our average flight approximates just one hour, we offer reserved but open seating in our comfortable single class 737 cabin.

Additionally, our inflight service is simplified because meals are neither practical nor necessary.

Our fare structure is the simplest in the domestic airline industry, and our Company Club frequent flyer program is also simple, generously rewarding our frequent flyers with free trips.

Consistent with our "keep it simple" approach, Southwest was the first major airline to introduce Ticketless Travel, which makes "ticketing" on Southwest even easier. Southwest's unique Ticketless system, which was fully implemented in January 1995, eliminates the inconvenience of acquiring a paper ticket. Currently, 35 percent of our Customers use Ticketless Travel, and we believe this percentage will grow as our Customers experience its ease and convenience. Our Customers will soon be able to book Southwest Ticketless Travel directly using our Home Page on the Internet (http://www.iflyswa.com). When it comes to technology and streamlining our operations, our Employees are on the leading edge.

While our approach may be simple, our Customer Satisfaction consistently ranks best in the industry because we deliver what the Customer wants in shorthaul markets.

"We believe simpler is always better. Most people's lives are complicated enough. Why add to their problems?"

— GARY A. BARRON
Executive Vice President-Chief Operations Officer

2

Keep it simple. Southwest Airlines honors some simple no-nos: No assigned seats. No meals. No hassles. No problems. Do our Customers like the way we do business? You could say they're simply nuts about it!

IMPRESSE WORKS **RARE, LTD.** ENGLAND

WHEN RARE FIRST SHOWED NINTENDO HOW THEY COULD INJECT NEW MAGIC INTO THE SUPER NES, NINTENDO AGREED TO LEND DONKEY KONG FOR A LEADING ROLE. THE RESULT: A STAGGERING PACE OF SALES WORLDWIDE, AND THE **MOST** POPULAR GAME SERIES OF THE 90'S. THIS YEAR, **BANJO-** A COMICAL HONEY BEAR AND HIS FUN-LOVING SIDEKICK, **KAZOOIE** ARE POISED TO BE THE BREAKTHROUGH STARS OF '97, REVOLUTIONIZING INTERACTIVE FUN BY INTRODUCING THE PLAYER, FOR THE FIRST TIME, TO THE UNIQUE PERSONALITY TRAITS OF THE GAME CHARACTERS.

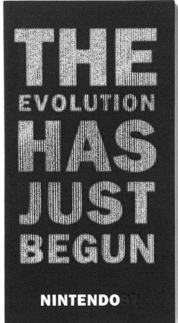

THE EVOLUTION HAS JUST BEGUN

NINTENDO 97

Design Firm: Leimer Cross Design Corporation
Creative Director, Art Director, Designer:
Kerry Leimer
Photographer: Tyler Boley
Illustrator: E3 Nintendo
Copywriters: Kerry Leimer, Don Varyu
Client: Nintendo of America

NINTENDO CHANGES THE BUSINESS

Design Firm: Cahan & Associates
Creative Director, Art Director: Bill Cahan
Designer: Kevin Roberson
Photographer: William McLeod
Copywriter: Thom Elkjer
Client: Xilinx, Inc.

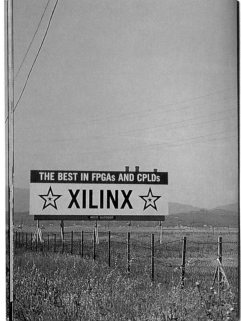

Capital Re Corporation and Subsidiaries
Financial Highlights

			Year ended December 31.		
[Dollars in thousands except per share amounts]	1996	1995	1994	1993	1992
Summary of Operations					
Gross Premiums Written	$ 125,818	$107,596	$94,861	$85,967	$79,283
Net Premiums Written	105,188	89,508	82,796	73,946	53,153
Net Premiums Earned	92,436	60,097	58,850	44,986	27,799
Net Investment Income	51,558	46,654	40,119	32,131	23,760
Net Realized Gains	1,471	53	1,780	881	5,487
Total Revenues	146,416	107,085	101,462	79,477	58,443
Net Income	56,524	45,527	39,806	36,354	30,153
Balance Sheet					
Investment Portfolio	901,192	771,767	638,751	552,405	443,688
Total Assets	1,156,401	981,885	810,040	711,633	608,547
Net Deferred Premium Revenue	265,070	252,318	222,907	198,860	147,079
Stockholders' Equity	489,846	411,943	325,514	323,832	270,593
Per Share Data					
Earnings Per Share	3.61	3.08	2.89	2.43	2.16
Book Value Per Share	30.86	27.82	22.02	21.66	18.71
Statutory Surplus and Reserves					
Unearned Premium Reserve	307,236	278,380	242,574	218,095	163,812
Contingency Reserve	123,963	89,685	63,591	43,459	94,472
Policyholders' Surplus	443,451	412,884	401,743	304,222	250,720
Total Policyholders' Surplus and Reserves	874,650	781,549	707,908	565,776	449,904

Design Firm: Donovan and Green
Creative Director, Art Director, Designer:
Clint Morgan
Photographer: Reven T.C. Wurman
Copywriter: Cathy Bailey
Client: Capital Re Corporation

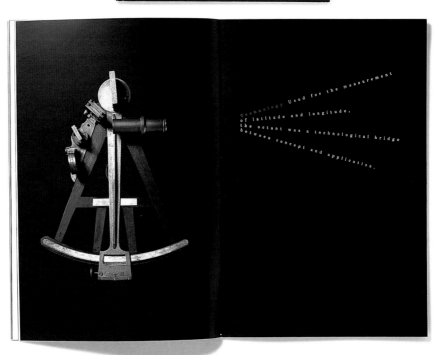

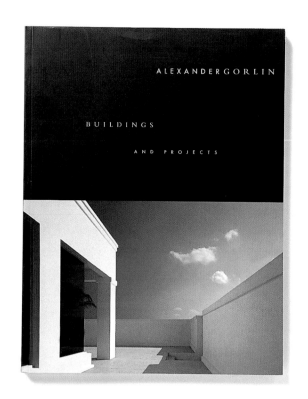

(top)
Design Firm: Pentagram Design
Art Director, Designer: Michael Bierut
Client: Rizzoli International

(middle)
Design Firm: Elixir Design
Creative Director: Jill Jacobson
Art Director: Jennifer Jerde
Designers: Jennifer Huff-Breeze,
Nathan Durrant, Michael Braley
Client: Chronicle Books/
Smithsonian Institute

(bottom)
Design Firm: Brad Norr Design
Designer: Brad Norr
Client: University of Minnesota Press

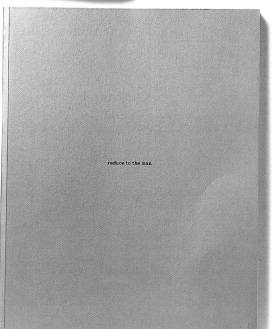

reduce to the max.

Design Firm: Weber, Hodel, Schmid
Advertising Ltd.
Creative Director: Beda Achermann
Art Directors: Marcus Bucher,
Ercole Troisi, Juerg Aemmer
Designers: Reinhold Weber, Yvonne Hodel,
Liliane Lerch, Thomas von An
Copywriter: Peter Ruch
Client: MCC Micro Compact Car

Islamic Arts Jonathan Bloom and Sheila Blair

ART & IDEAS

PHAIDON

Greek Art Nigel Spivey

ART & IDEAS

PHAIDON

Neoclassicism David Irwin

ART & IDEAS

PHAIDON

Dali Robert Radford

ART & IDEAS

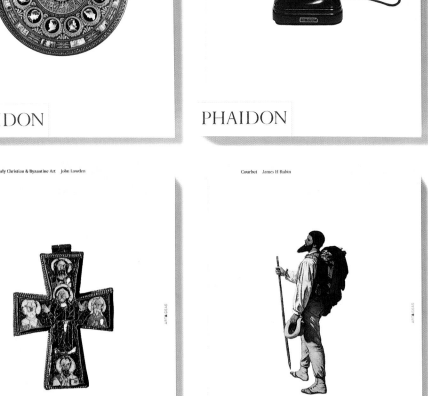

PHAIDON

Early Christian & Byzantine Art John Lowden

ART & IDEAS

PHAIDON

Courbet James H Rubin

ART & IDEAS

PHAIDON

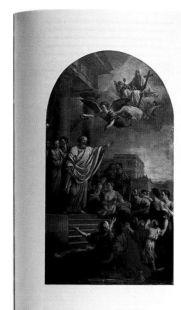

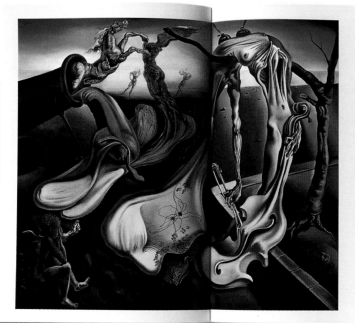

AESTHETICS AND TABOO:

DEALING WITH CULTURAL, RELIGIOUS MYTHS ALSO IMPLIES ADDRESSING SOCIAL TABOOS AT THE SAME TIME. WE NEED ONLY REMEMBER THE HEFTY CONTROVERSIES SURROUNDING THE PICTURES BY ROBERT MAPPLETHORPE, SALLY MANN, JOCK STURGES OR ANDRES SERRANO. REPRESENTATIONS OF THE BODY THAT TRANSGRESS CONVENTIONAL IDEAS ALWAYS INCITE A PASSIONATE RESPONSE FROM THE PUBLIC, ESPECIALLY THOSE REPRE-SENTATIONS THAT CONCERN QUESTIONS OF DEATH AND SEXUALITY.

The display of sickness and death (which are taboo topics specifically because they are not mentioned, concealed) is especially an element of the work of photographic artists, such as the New York based artist Matuschka. Following a breast amputation necessitated by cancer and medical diagnosis, she consciously displayed her partially destroyed, but otherwise painfully intact body as the destruction of the wound consti-

tuting it - on the threshold of aestheticizing that which is not capable of being aestheticized, she uses her own body to demonstrate not an image of her body, but the corporeal lies of images that do not show transience and infirmity. The ensuing shock does not result primarily from the view of the metonymy of a beautiful and partially destroyed body, but rather from a deeper and more lashing source, from the compelling awareness of the destructibility and

the social relevance of beauty. Another contemporary artistic strategy that takes up the challenge of attempting to remove taboos may be found in the work of Mapplethorpe and Serrano, for example. Both use the aesthetization of violence and death, in other words, an affirmation of destruction, although in different ways: Mapplethorpe through his aggressive language of forms and Serrano through the concept of aestheticizing death. The way in

which Gerhard Merzeder deals with taboos is positioned in between the strategies mentioned here, between bringing into view and aestheticizing. The theme of death or physical decay is so obviously staged that it subverts the voyeuristic gaze. Yet it is precisely this artificial staging that shows even more clearly the painful proximity of beauty and destruction.

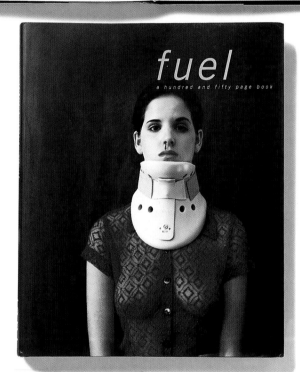

(previous spread)
Design Firm: Phaidon Press Limited (in-house)
Art Director: Alan Fletcher
Designers: Quentin Newark, John Powner, Phil Barnes
Client: Phaidon Press Limited

(this page)
Design Firm: Fotonerkstatt (in-house)
Art Director, Creative Director: Sigi Mayer
Photographer: Gerhard Merzeder
Client: Fotonerkstatt

Design Firm: Festo Corporate Design
Client: Festo AG+Co.
Designers: Martin Danzer,
Roman Riedmüller, Axel Thallemer

(left)
Design Firm: Sargent & Berman
Creative Director: Peter Sargent
Art Director: David Vostmyer
Designer: Rene Pulve
Copywriter: Carol Doumani
Client: Wave Publishing

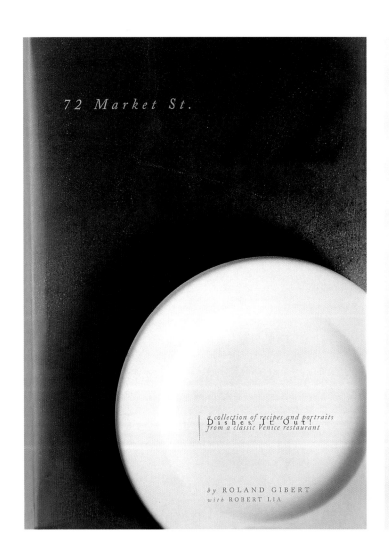

72 Market St.

a collection of recipes and portraits
Dishes It Out!
from a classic Venice restaurant

by ROLAND GIBERT
with ROBERT LIA

Paul Auster

The Music of Chance

A Novel

(right, opposite page)
Design Firm: Hans-Heinrich Sures
Photographer: Arne Pastoor

Jay McInerney

Story of my Life

A Novel

andrew vachss
blossom

roman·ullstein

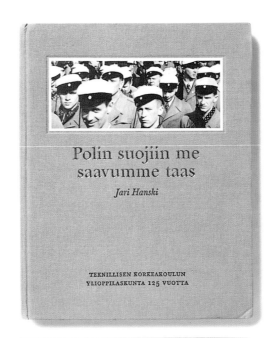

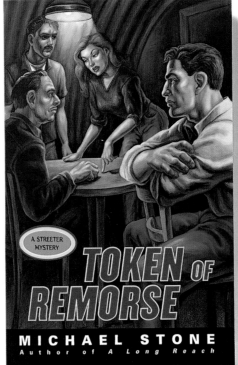

(top)
Design Firm: Marko Myllyluoma
Art Director: Marko Myllyluoma
Client: Teknillisen Korkeakoulun/
Ylioppilas Kunta

(middle)
Design Firm: Penguin Putnam,
Inc. (in-house)
Art Director: Paul Buckley
Designer: Roseanne Serra
Illustrator: Owen Smith
Client: Penguin Putnam, Inc.

(bottom)
Design Firm: Random House, Inc.
(in-house)
Art Director: Robbin Schiff
Designer: Gabrielle Bordwin
Photographer: Maurice Weiss/Ostkrevz
Client: Random House, Inc.

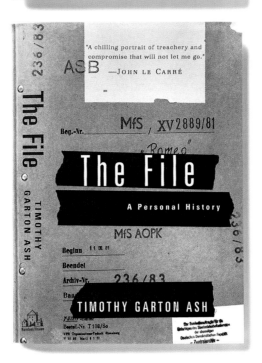

"This boy is not our usual type of hero.
He is all the others rolled into
one and multiplied by ten . . ."
—WILL ROGERS

▶ CHARLES LINDBERGH 1902–1974

▲ JOHN GLENN 1921–

"This guy had the halo turned on at all times!"
—TOM WOLFE

52

Design Firm: Life Magazine (in-house)
Art Director: Tom Bentkowski,
Sharon Okamoto
Designer: Sharon Okamoto
Client: Life Magazine

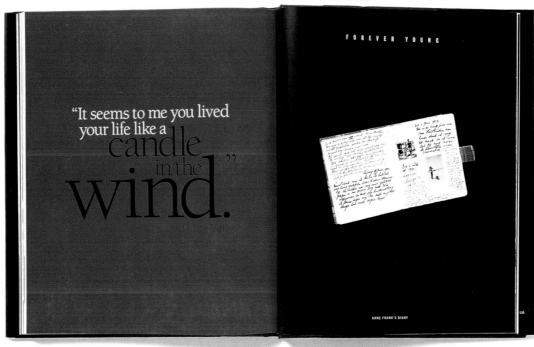

FOREVER YOUNG

"It seems to me you lived
your life like a
candle
in the
wind."

ANNE FRANK'S DIARY

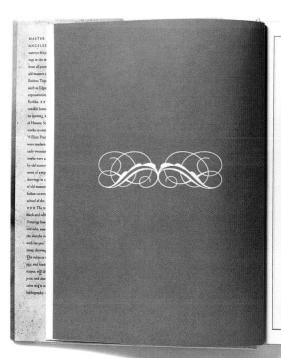

Designer: Amy McFarland
Client: Los Angeles County
Museum of Art

(opposite)
Design Firm: Callaway Editions
(in-house)
Creative Director: Nicholas Callaway
Designer: Toshiya Masuda
Illustrator: David Kirk
Editor: Antoinette White
Client: Scholastic, Inc.

Poor Holley shrieked, "It's much too fast!
Please look out where you're going.
There might be hungry rats down there.
We have no way of knowing."
"How fine it is," Miss Spider laughed,
"To feel my toppy blowing!"

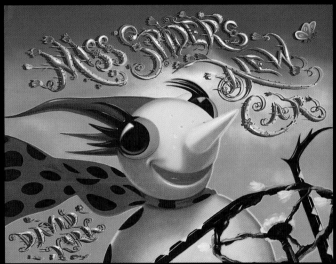

Beneath the door, upon the floor,
Miss Spider found a note.
"Another message from my mom,
I wonder what she wrote. . . .

Design Firm: Carre Noir
Creative Director, Designer:
Andrew Pengilly
Art Director: Michael Disle
Photographer: Robin Barton
Client: Tag Heuer S.A.

(opposite)
Design Firm: Sayles Graphic Design
Art Director, Designer, Illustrator:
John Sayles
Photographer: John Clark
Printer: Artcraft
Client: Hotel Pattee

Design Firm: Tom Fowler, Inc.
Creative Director, Art Director:
Thomas Fowler
Designer: Karl S. Maruyama
Photographer: Tod Bryant/Shooters, Inc.
Client: UIS, Inc.

U IS is a privately held corporation with assets of more than $700 million and a family of companies whose growth records place them among the leaders in the industries they serve. Our business is acquiring solid, well-managed companies in specific manufacturing segments and providing them with the capital, expertise and other resources they need to grow sales and profits. We encourage the teams in charge at the time of acquisition to stay on board and continue building company success.

Who Is UIS?

Our three primary areas of focus are automotive and truck parts, millwork, and confectionery products. UIS companies include many of the most widely known and respected names in these fields. Our approach has always been to let UIS companies build on their own identities without trying to re-make them as scions of a corporate parent.

Though we employ approximately 9,000 people in the United States and Europe, the UIS corporate office in Jersey City, New Jersey consists of only fifteen people. We do not need a larger group because of our strategy of acquiring companies that require minimal corporate oversight and then allowing their managers to continue growing sales and profit.

We believe there is no substitute for the ideas, skills and energy of the people running successful businesses. That is why UIS continues to re-invest not only in current operations but also in new companies that complement and extend our many strengths.

Hurd's "heat mirror" windows reflect the heat and cold, helping homes and other structures stay warmer in the winter and cooler in the summer. To manufacture the windows, Hurd developed new production processes and built new manufacturing lines, funding the process with UIS capital.

Because of the autonomy that Hurd enjoys, the company attracts talented engineers looking for fertile ground for developing visionary new concepts, like those that led to the "heat mirror" window.

New construction or retrofit? Hurd's ability to profitably serve both markets with technologically advanced products has helped it keep sales on the rise even when the housing start cycle has dipped.

Millwork

Hurd Millwork Company is an industry leader in the manufacture of high-performance windows, patio doors, frames and, through its Stair Parts subsidiary, spindles, balustrades and other millwork. The company markets to wholesale outlets in the United States and approximately 20 other countries.

Hurd's industry leadership extends to setting nationwide standards for windows through its active membership in the National Fenestration Rating Council, an organization that is instrumental in shaping building codes across the country.

Hurd has a long tradition of craftsmanship dating back to the company's founding in 1922.

When Ken Hallgren became president of Hurd in 1974, it was largely a manufacturer of commodity window components. Hallgren led the company into an era of great technological change and pioneering developments in energy-efficient, low-maintenance windows and doors. "The independence that corporate gives us is tremendous," he says. "It allowed Hurd to remake itself as the company that tries new things, the source for unique and superior products."

Production capacity at Stair Parts was limited by cramped quarters and outdated equipment. Then the company was acquired by UIS, enabling it to buy a new, 110,000-square-foot plant and furnish it with computer-controlled routers. Both quality and productivity are now on the rise as are sales and profits.

In 1996 Hurd set up a state-of-the-art plant to manufacture a new line of high-performance vinyl windows. By paying careful attention to product quality and engineering, Hurd has established itself as a leader in energy efficiency, design flexibility and product durability in the vinyl window marketplace as well.

U IS is interested in finding public or private companies priced at up to $150 million to complement its existing businesses and further the growth of the entire corporation. Specifically, we seek manufacturing companies in three sectors: Automobile and truck parts (aftermarket and original equipment manufacturing); millwork, as well as other types of wooden building products or components; and confectionery, including boxed chocolates, bars, bagged items and specialties.

Joining UIS.

We would also consider manufacturers of products similar to those listed above and not requiring high technology or heavy R&D outlays. Stand-alone annual sales should be at least $10 million, with no size limit on product acquisitions that can be incorporated into an existing business. We favor North American or Western European firms but will consider those located elsewhere.

We are not interested in turnaround situations, or in retail, service, real estate, banking, insurance, natural resources or high technology companies. We prefer to conduct our own negotiations. All information is treated in strict confidence.

For more information on UIS and the opportunities it might hold for your company, we invite you to contact Richard J. Pasculano, Executive Vice President, at 203.861.2784 (fax 203.861.2786).

Financial Highlights

Joseph F. Arrigo
Executive Vice President and Treasurer
Primarily responsible for the financial evaluation of our operating companies, accounting functions, as well as tax and acquisition matters. Mr. Arrigo draws on over 40 years of experience in corporate financial management.

Melvin Spencer
Senior Executive Vice President
Mr. Spencer understands both the needs of acquired companies and the role of UIS management. He was a key member of the Airtex management team when the company was acquired by UIS, became its President and now, is our divisional administrator responsible for supervising our automotive and other manufacturing operations.

Thomas W. Mellars
Vice President
Mr. Mellars, a CPA with over 20 years of experience in both public and private accounting, adds depth and strength to the UIS corporate team. An MBA in Finance, Mr. Mellars is responsible for assisting in the evaluation of accounting, tax and acquisition matters.

Andrew G. Pietrini
Chairman, President and CEO
Mr. Pietrini has 30 years of experience in both corporate finance and general management, and has played a central role in the company's financial management and evaluation of new acquisitions.

Richard J. Pasculano
Executive Vice President
Mr. Pasculano is a broadly experienced corporate executive and draws on over 30 years of experience with UIS. He is currently responsible for the company's merger and acquisitions program.

UIS

Corporate Officers

Design Firm: Axcess Group
Art Director: Brent McMahon
Designers: Lionel Ferreira,
Jeremy Wirth
Photographer: Roland Bishop
Copywriter: Tony King
Client: Masland Contract

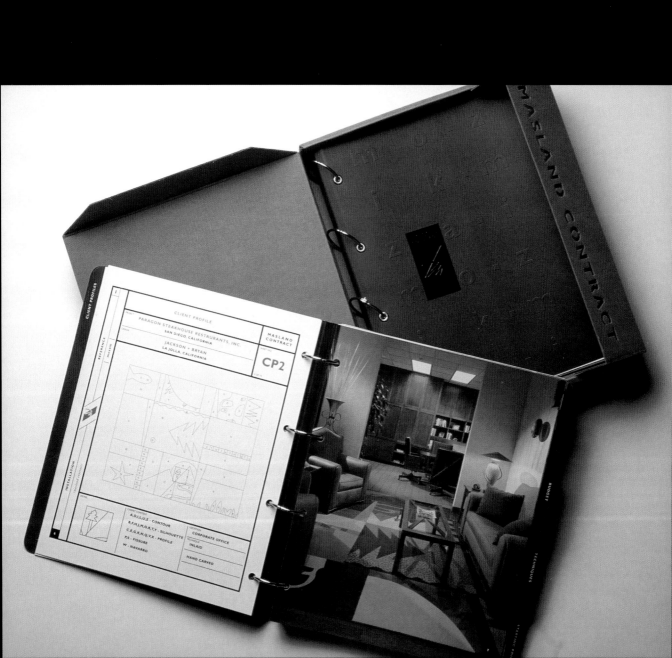

The R.L. Winston Rod Company

Since 1929, Winston has been dedicated to making the finest fly rods in the world. For a number of years, the company was based in San Francisco; since 1976, it's been in the small town of Twin Bridges, Montana, pretty much within casting distance of the Beaverhead, Ruby, Jefferson and Big Hole rivers.

There's a lot of history and tradition behind the Winston name. And it has always been a source of pride to those who have worked here that our rods are so treasured by anglers.

1929 After the stock market crash, the Western Fishing Rod Company, located in San Francisco, is acquired by Robert Winther and Lew Stoner. They call their rods "Winston," a combination of the two men's last names. The company soon becomes known for its outstanding bamboo rods.

1933 Robert Winther sells his interest to an employee, Walter "Red" Loskot. Loskot is an accomplished fisherman and member of the Golden Gate Angling and Casting Club.

1934 Lew Stoner develops a hollow-fluted rod design for use in tournament casting competitions. The Winston built with this design wins lightweight, very powerful, and would soon shatter a number of world distance casting records.

1936 Promi Lisman uses a Winston surf rod to break the world record with a 623 foot cast. In 1938, Marcus Hedge uses a Winston to break the world fly casting record for 56 feet.

1945 Doug Merrick steps into the shop to buy a rod. Instead, the future owner of Winston finds a job.

1950's Loskot sells his interest to Merrick in 1953. Stoner dies in 1957, leaving Merrick as the sole owner. Winston begins using a new material to make rods: fiberglass.

1967 Charles Ritz, President of the International Fario Club in Paris, presents Merrick with a medal this year for his "Outstanding work and knowledge pertaining to split bamboo fly rods."

1973 Tom Morgan buys Winston from Doug Merrick, continuing the company's tradition of craftsmanship and innovative design.

1974 Glenn Brackett comes to work at Winston, and soon becomes a partner. The company also introduces the "Stalker" series, a line of specialized fiberglass rods developed for making delicate presentations on challenging rivers and spring creeks.

Above, R.L. Winston 9 1/2-foot bamboo steelhead rod, circa 1950, built by Lew Stoner.

Right, Patent drawings for Lew Stoner's hollow-fluted rod design.

1975 Winston first offers a line of graphite rods.

1976 In order to be near the world-class trout fishing of the Beaverhead, Ruby, Jefferson and Big Hole rivers, Morgan and Brackett move the company from San Francisco to Twin Bridges, Montana.

1987 Winston introduces a new line of rods made from IM6 graphite.

1991 David Ondaatje buys the company from Morgan and Brackett, and works closely with both in order to continue the Winston heritage of fine rod design.

1994 Winston begins rolling its own graphite blanks, providing the company with an even greater degree of quality control. Also this year, rods made with LT graphite are introduced.

1995 Winston moves to a new, larger rodbuilding shop in Twin Bridges.

1996 Winston's 5-piece LT trout rods are introduced. Joan Wulff joins Winston as a technical advisor.

1997 The Joan Wulff Favorite, a rod designed specifically to meet the needs of women anglers, is introduced.

1998 The company develops a new line of 5-piece, fast action saltwater rods. Called BLS, they're made with a revolutionary boron/graphite composite.

R.L. Winston Rod Co., 1998

R.L. WINSTON ROD CO.

The rainbow trout of a lifetime. Or a permit tailing seventy feet away. These are one cast situations, moments of truth, and times when you will appreciate having a Winston in your hand. Winstons are light, they are balanced. They are designed to make smooth casts and delicate fly presentations. They are built to inspire confidence and, ultimately, to catch fish.

LIEBE.
BEGEHRTHEIT.
ERFOLG
UND
E W I G E
JUGEND.

COME
B A C K
EINER GROSSEN
LIEBE.

Design Firm: Michael Osborne Design
Art Director: Michael Osborne
Designer: Paul Kagiwada
Client: Tayland Cellars

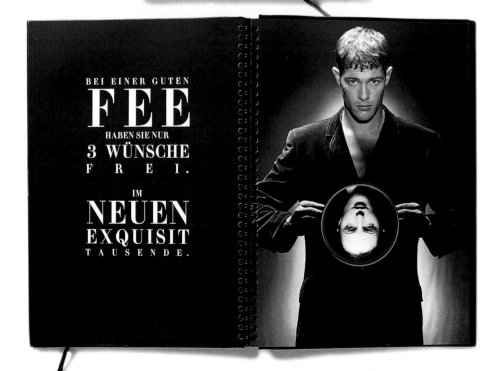

BEI EINER GUTEN
FEE
HABEN SIE NUR
3 WÜNSCHE
F R E I.
IM
NEUEN
EXQUISIT
T A U S E N D E.

> "Life is like software.
> Version upgrades
> are available."

God bless the computer. Thanks to this wonderful tool, all of the processes that contribute to the realization of the literature we print, and the responsibilities of the people who create them – and who hire Bell Press – have changed forever. ◆ Modern hardware and software have given us new tools and new freedom, and has even helped transform the way many graphic designers think and see things. Sophisticated facets of the print production process formerly trusted only to highly trained, experienced and exacting pre-press experts are now in the hands of desktop publishers at their computer terminals. ◆ There's been a dynamic change in the workflow process that's begun to cloud the lines of responsibility. ◆ And unfortunately, along with the promise of more control, cost effectiveness and time savings, digitally prepared files can also leave the door wide open for misinterpretations, miscommunications, unforeseen headaches, missed deliveries and overtime expenses that might eat up the savings you could realize by doing a lot of the work yourself. ◆ To help prevent that from happening (and because we're good guys), we've prepared this booklet addressing many of the more common oversights made by people preparing and supplying electronic layouts and pre-press specs. It attempts to set forth an easy-to-follow set of standards to ensure clear communications between Bell Press and the growing number of clients who choose to prepare their layouts and mechanicals on the computer. ◆ Please read it. And refer to it when preparing your files. ◆ I hope the information contained on the following pages will make you say, "God bless the computer." (Instead of something else.) **Scott Harvin**

Design Firm: DBD International, Ltd.
Art Director, Designer, Illustrator: David Brier
Copywriter: Al Gorman
Client: Bell Press Incorporated

CALL BELL PRESS FIRST, SO WE WON'T HAVE TO CALL YOU LATER

Perhaps the simplest way to avoid potential electronic file prep problems is to involve Bell Press in the pre-planning stages. By picking up the phone and calling one of our tech-heads before preparing your files, questions can be answered and many potential problems can be eliminated. So, if after reading this booklet you remember nothing else, at least remember one thing. Our number: 973 759 2334.

A FEW FACTS ABOUT
FONTS

The Adobe Postscript language has given rise to beautiful typography created on the computer. But to realize the results you expect, there are a few precautions you'll need to follow....

Use Type One™ Fonts. Experience has shown that TrueType™ fonts don't always image correctly on modern image setting equipment. If you happen to have TrueType fonts in your system, it's best to replace them with Type One versions as soon as possible to avoid problems. Be careful not to throw away the fonts that come with your system (Symbol, Courier, Geneva, Chicago, Cairo, etc.) as some of them are needed by the computer to accomplish everyday tasks.

Always provide copies of the fonts you used. Numbering conventions can change between vendors and cause conflicts so it's best to send copies of the screen and printer fonts you've used to us along with your job. Be sure to also include the fonts used in imported EPS illustration files as well. These won't appear in the QuarkXpress™ or Pagemaker™ "Font Usage" windows but are still in your EPS files

Avoid using automated style attribute buttons to achieve bold, italic, outline, shadow, etc.. These are antiquated commands from the days when there weren't too many font options and many of the newer image setting machines and printer drivers ignore these pseudo software attributes So, to get the style you want, use only font styles of the actual fonts you have on your hard drive (e.g., "Garamond Bold Italic").

Supply a list of all fonts used. This will help expedite the process of opening and loading your fonts before actually opening and processing your document files. A font list can be compiled easily and automatically using the QuarkXpress's "Collect for Output" feature.

SOUVENIR ALBUMS

Once easy to find at flea markets
and antique fairs, promotional souvenir albums
produced by the thousands in
the late 19th century have become scarce,
since most owners did not value
them the way they did published books.
This collection was put together over the years by
San Francisco designer Linda Hinrichs,
who found them intriguing both from an historical
and graphic standpoint.

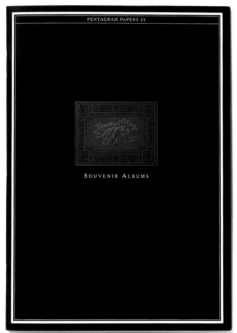

SOUVENIR ALBUMS

Design Firm: Michael Osborne Design
Creative Director, Designer:
Michael Osborne
Client: San Francisco Museum
of Modern Art (SFMOMA)

Completion of the transcontinental railroad in 1869 and celebration of the United States Centennial in 1876 boosted American tourism in the late 19th century and stimulated national pride. Travelers clamored for souvenir pictures of places they had visited, and proud Americans sought mementos of historic national achievements to display in their parlors.

With halftone printing and hand-held cameras yet to be introduced, U.S. publishers collaborated with printers in Germany to convert photographs or drawings into stone lithographic reproductions. Between 1870 and 1915, this roundabout method resulted in thousands of souvenir albums featuring American landmarks, scenic views and national events. Competition to produce these miniature albums – typically 3½ x 4 inches to 6¼ x 9½ inches in size – became so feverish in the 1880s that The American Bookmaker described this "summer resort printing" as a "war of the monotint booklet." Until recently scholars dismissed the value of these tiny albums, but today researchers recognize their documentary importance, and museums and libraries are beginning to collect and catalog them. Fascinating not only for their historical content, these albums mark a transitional period in the development of photography, design and lithography.

[SEE THE WORLD BY RAIL]

Railways opened up the American frontier and made it
possible for common folks to see the continent in relative comfort.
Sold or given away at railroad depots, luggage shops
and stationers, souvenir albums catered to this new market by touting
the modern mode of transportation the traveler was likely
to enjoy and the scenic and cultural highlights – and sometimes
the major hotels – along the route.

NEW YORK AND BROOKLYN BRIDGE.

[LEISURE CLASS TRAVEL]

In the days when passenger steamships plied the Atlantic coastal waters, shipping lines used souvenir albums to attract the Victorian leisure class. Like today's cruise line promotions,

this 1894 album for the Fall River Line showcased a profile view of the ship, exciting ports-of-call like New York City (with the newly built Brooklyn Bridge in the foreground) and well-dressed passengers enjoying luxurious accommodations.

[EXOTIC FAR WEST]

Even at the start of the 20th century, Los Angeles had a reputation for being strange and exotic - a real attraction for adventurous travelers from the East and Midwest. In addition to showcasing mansions, beach-front hotels and public buildings, this viewbook offered an intriguing look at some of the region's unusual flora and fauna. Land developers also used the album to cast the territory in a positive light and counter its reputation for being a waterless, desert plain.

Inexpensive photographic postcards and Brownie cameras that any tourist could use brought an end to the era of souvenir albums. During their brief appearance, American souvenir albums with their near photographic-quality images provided the public with the first realistic view of the world outside their physical environs—and what an awesome sight it was.

PENTAGRAM PAPERS 25

Pentagram Papers will publish examples of curious, entertaining, stimulating, provocative and occasionally controversial points of view that have come to the attention of, or in some cases are actually originated by, Pentagram.

Photography: Bob Esparza
Text: Delphine Hirasuna

Surf's up.

SLK

This transmission has got you figured out. It won't take long for the SLK's driver-adaptive electronically controlled 5-speed automatic to get you down cold. Go ahead and drive the way you've always imagined driving a roadster. Let your right foot dance the tango with the gas pedal, stepping gently at times, pressing swiftly to the floor at other times, lifting suddenly when the situation calls for it. You'll be amazed how much it feels in sync with your driving desires. This is, as *Car and Driver* attests, "a fascinating machine that is better able to change its character to match the mood of the driver than any other sports car."

SLK 230 shown with accessory 5-spoke wheels available through your Mercedes-Benz dealer.

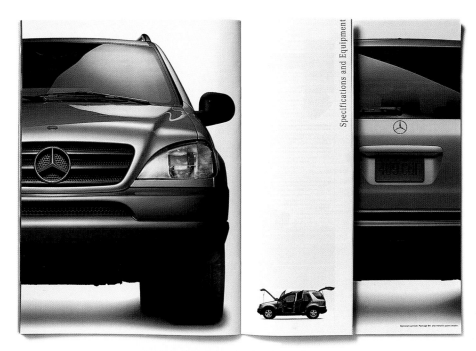

Specifications and Equipment

Design Firm: The Designory, Inc.
Art Director, Designer:
Andrea Schindler
Photographers: Vic Huber,
Michael Rausch
Copywriters: Theo Wallace,
Rich Conklin
Client: Mercedes–Benz
of North America

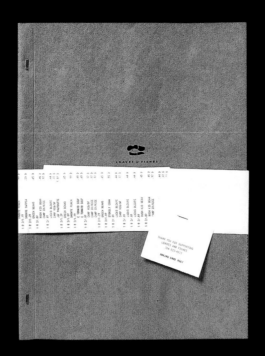

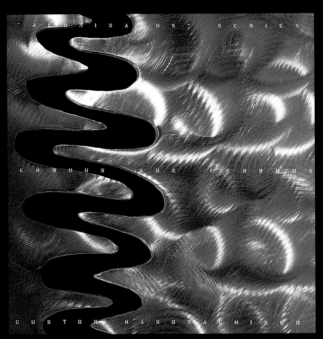

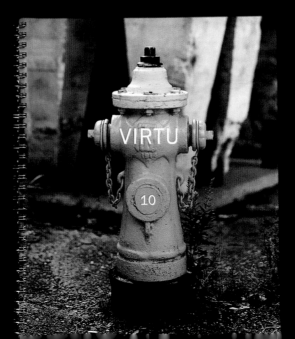

(opposite, top)
Design Firm:
BlackBird Creative
Creative Director: Patrick Short
Designer: Kristy Beausoleil
Photographer: Brad Bridgers
Copywriter: Brad Bray
Client: Loaves & Fishes

(opposite middle, this page)
Design Firm: LBC Design, Inc.
Creative Directors: Bob Lukens,
Scott Clark, Ken Boostrom
Designer: Scott Clark
Photographer: Glen Turner
Copywriter: Peter Nourjain
Client: Ferrous Non Ferrous

(opposite, bottom)
Design Firm: Concrete Design
Communications Inc.
Art Directors: Diti Katona, John Pylypczak
Designer: Nick Monteleone
Photographer: Ron Baxter Smith
Copywriter: Esther Shipman
Client: Virtu

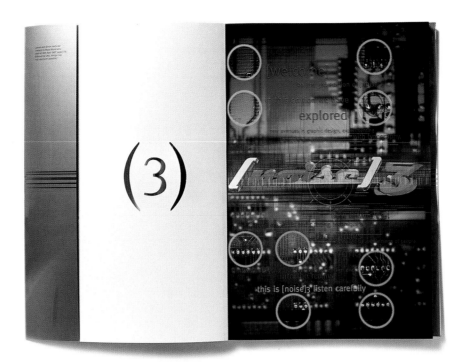

Design Firm: The Attik (in-house)
Client: The Attik

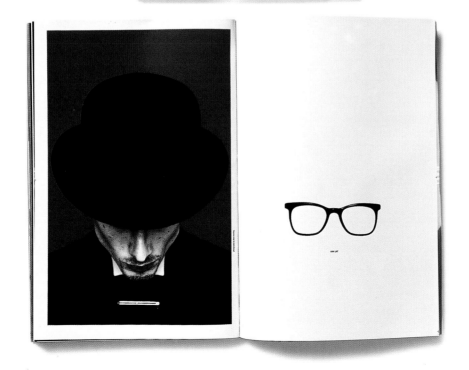

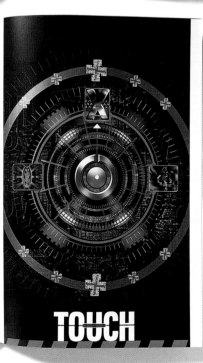

I am living proof that early detection provides the best opportunity to survive breast cancer. Three years ago a mammogram revealed a suspicious mass in my breast. I could hardly believe it, because I felt so good. I was treated at the Beth Israel Deaconess BreastCare Center, where a team of healthcare professionals guided me through all my procedures. The center is dedicated to the detection and treatment of breast cancer and provides a complete range of diagnostic and treatment services, including mammograms. In a single session the multidisciplinary BreastCare Program brings together world-class surgeons, radiologists, medical and radiation oncologists, nurses and pathologists to review each case individually. This unique program gave me a high sense of confidence.

My husband, John, was my biggest supporter during the most difficult time in my life.

Design Firm:
Haggman Advertising
Creative Director,
Copywriter: Eric Haggman
Art Director,
Designer: Amy Farr
Photographer: David Zadig
Client: Beth Israel Hospital

How can I have Cancer, when I feel so good? (One woman's story.)

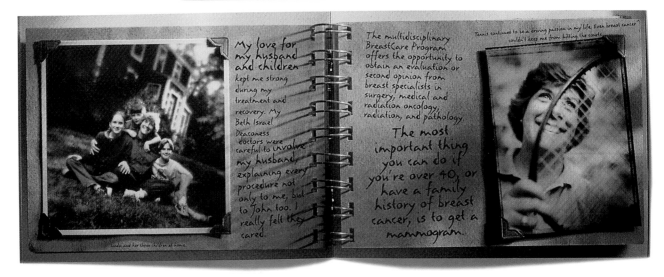

My love for my husband and children kept me strong during my treatment and recovery. My Beth Israel Deaconess doctors were careful to involve my husband, explaining every procedure not only to me, but to John too. I really felt they cared.

Linda and her three children at home.

The multidisciplinary BreastCare Program offers the opportunity to obtain an evaluation or second opinion from breast specialists in surgery, medical and radiation oncology, radiation, and pathology.

The most important thing you can do if you're over 40, or have a family history of breast cancer, is to get a mammogram.

Tennis continues to be a driving passion in my life. Even breast cancer couldn't keep me from hitting the courts.

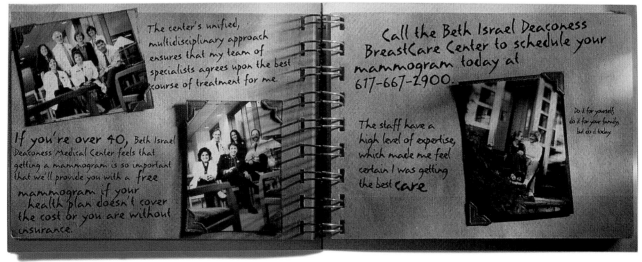

The center's unified, multidisciplinary approach ensures that my team of specialists agrees upon the best course of treatment for me.

If you're over 40, Beth Israel Deaconess Medical Center feels that getting a mammogram is so important that we'll provide you with a free mammogram if your health plan doesn't cover the cost, or you are without insurance.

Call the Beth Israel Deaconess BreastCare Center to schedule your mammogram today at 617-667-2900.

The staff have a high level of expertise, which made me feel certain I was getting the best care.

Do it for yourself, do it for your family, but do it today.

(top, middle)
Design Firm: Robertson Design
Art Director: John Robertson,
Jeff Carroll
Designer: Jeff Carroll
Photographer:Darrien Caughorn
Copywriter: Michael Nolan
Client: Patterson Press

(bottom)
Design Firm: Mullen Advertising
Art Director, Designer: Ginger Hood
Copywriter: Vashti Brotherhood
Printer: We Andrews
Client: Osram Sylvania

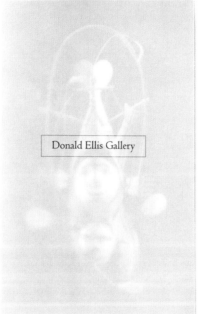

Donald Ellis Gallery

Design Firm: Hambley & Wooley Inc.
Creative Director: Bob Hambly
Art Director: Barb Woolley
Designer: Mercedes Rothwell
Client: Donald Ellis Gallery

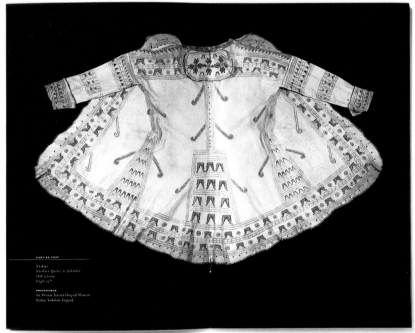

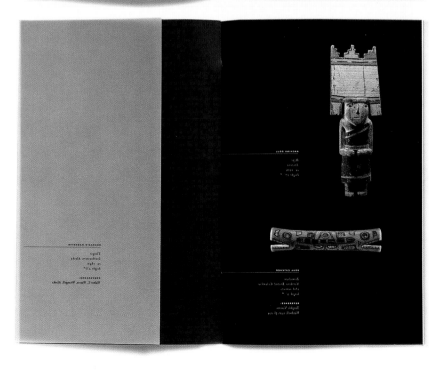

Design Firm: Fossil Design Studio
Art Director: Tim Hale
Designer: Casey McGarr
Client: Fossil

AUTHENTIC
FOSSIL®
GENUINE

THE

Original

"Don't look
any further"

CLASSIC

December

SUN	MON	TUE	WED	THU	FRI	SAT
	1	2	3	4	5	6
7	8	9	10	11	12	13
14	15	16	17	18	19	20
21	22	23	24	25	26	27
28	29	30	31			

January
1998

February

SUN	MON	TUE	WED	THU	FRI	SAT
1	2	3	4	5	6	7
8	9	10	11	12	13	14
15	16	17	18	19	20	21
22	23	24	25	26	27	28

SUN	MON	TUE	WED	THU	FRI	SAT
				1 New Year's Day	2	3
4	5	6	7	8	9	10
11	12	13	14	15	16	17
18	19 Martin Luther Kings, Jr's Birthday Observed	20	21	22	23	24
25	26	27	28	29	30	31

Jan 14, 1954, Actress Marilyn Monroe and former center fielder Joe DiMaggio wed this afternoon in San Francisco.

The New American Classic

The Watch In The Famous Tin Box

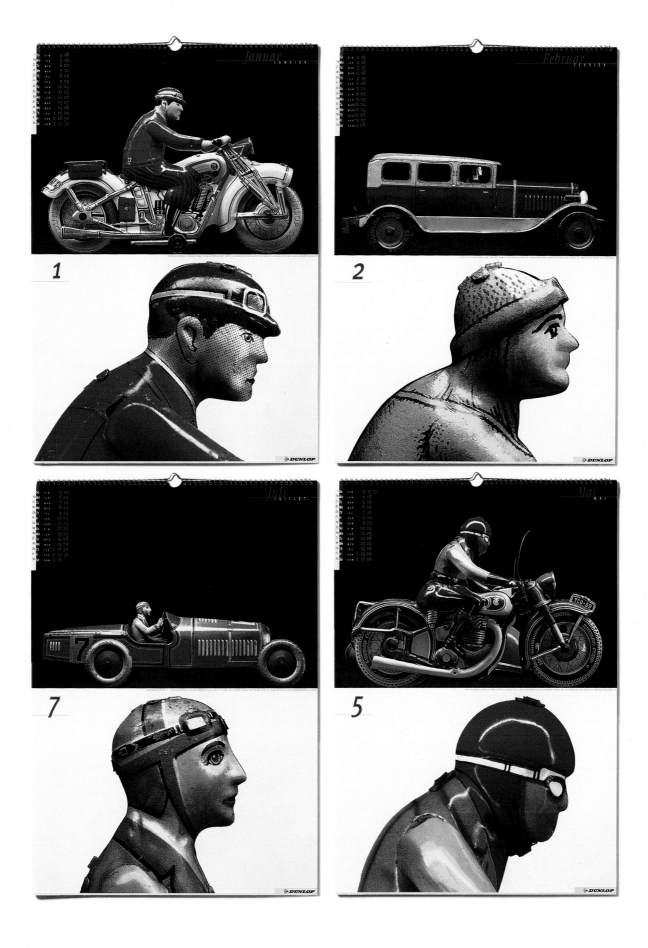

Design Firm: Atelier für Kommunikation
Art Director, Designer: Peter Shäublin
Peter Schäublin
Photographer: Per-Erik Berglund
Client: Znapshot AB

(opposite)
Design Firm: Bianco & Cucco
Art Directors, Designers:
Giovanni Bianco, Susanna Cucco
Photographer: Marco Pietracupa
Client: Triton Industria e Comércio
de Modas Ltda.

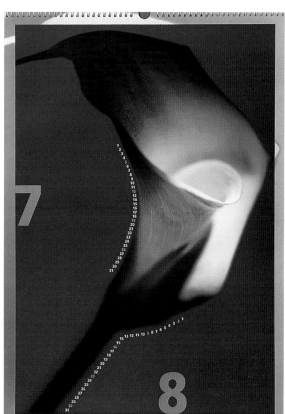

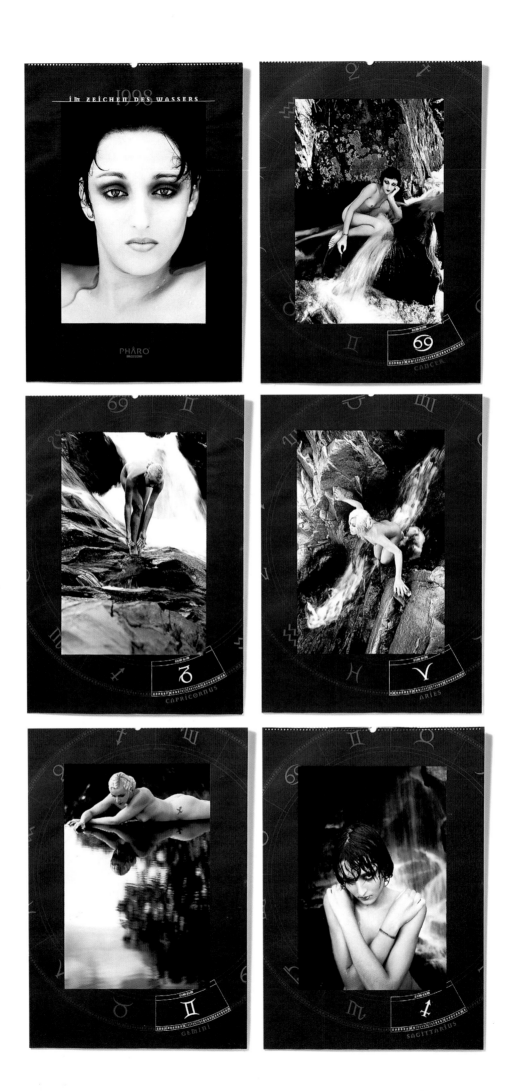

Design Firm: Wehrbung, Etc.
Designer: Stephanie Kreber
Photographer: Thomas Kettner
Client: Hansgrohe, Pharo Marketing

HORST HAMANN NEW YORK VERTICAL

august

HORST HAMANN NEW YORK VERTICAL

december

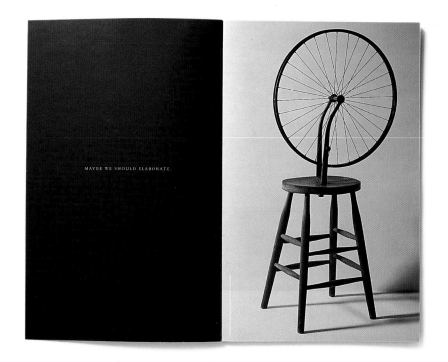

MAYBE WE SHOULD ELABORATE.

JUST BECAUSE A BIKE IS MADE BY HAND,
DOESN'T MEAN YOU'D WANT TO RIDE IT.

Design Firm: Cahan & Associates
Client: Trek Bicycles
Creative Director, Art Director: Bill Cahan
Designer: Bob Dinetz
Photographer: Robert Schlatter
Copywriter: Lisa Jhung

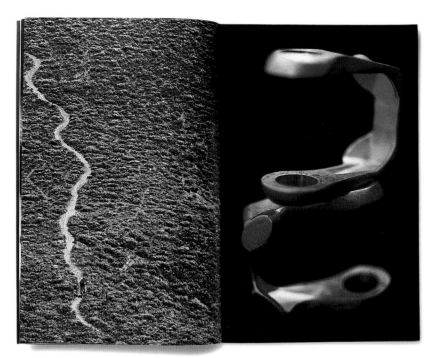

MANTRA PRO™

SIZES	S, M, L
FRAME	Klein Power Tubing main beam, Gradient stays
SUSPENSION	Rock Shox 100 65mm travel or Fox Alps 50 in
DRIVETRAIN	Shimano XTR Rapid Rise
PEDALS	Time ATAC Carbon clipless
WHEELS	Cane Creek CrossMomo
BRAKESET	XTR v-brakes
WEIGHT	24.8 lbs. (11.2kg) Made in Chehalis, Washington

MANTRA RACE LT™

SIZES	S, M, L
FRAME	Klein Power Tubing main beam, Gradient stays
SUSPENSION	Manitou x-vert e 100mm travel or Fox Alps 50 in
DRIVETRAIN	Shimano XT & XTR m 2nd & XT Rapid Fire to shiften
PEDALS	Time ATAC Carbon clipless
RIMS	Bontrager Mustang 10770 ours
BRAKESET	Hayes Hydraulic Disk or XT v-brake m
WEIGHT	28.9 lbs. (13.2kg) Made in Chehalis, Washington

ATTITUDE COMP™

SIZES	XS, S, M, L, XL
FRAME	Klein Gradient tools and stays
SUSPENSION	Rock Shox Judy SL 63/80/25 travel
DRIVETRAIN	Shimano XT & XTR m XT shiften
PEDALS	Time ATAC clipless
RIMS	Bontrager Mustang 1070 ours
BRAKESET	Avid single digit 20 direct pull
WEIGHT	24.2 lbs. (11kg) Made in Chehalis, Washington

Design Firm: Larsen Design + Interactive
Creative Director: Tim Larsen
Art Director: Donna Root
Designers: David Schultz, Wendy Ruyle
Illustrator: David Schultz
Copywriter: 2 Heads Communication
Printer: Diversified Graphics
Client: Novellus Systems, Inc.

(opposite)
Design Firm: Phoenix Creative
Art Director, Designer: Reid Thompson
Printer: Reprox of St. Louis
Client: Gregg Goldman

Design Firm: Larsen Design + Interactive
Creative Director: Tim Larsen
Art Director: Donna Root
Designers: Peter de Sibour, Sascha Boecker
Copywriter: 2 Heads Communications/Novellus
Printer: Diversified Graphics
Client: Novellus Systems, Inc.

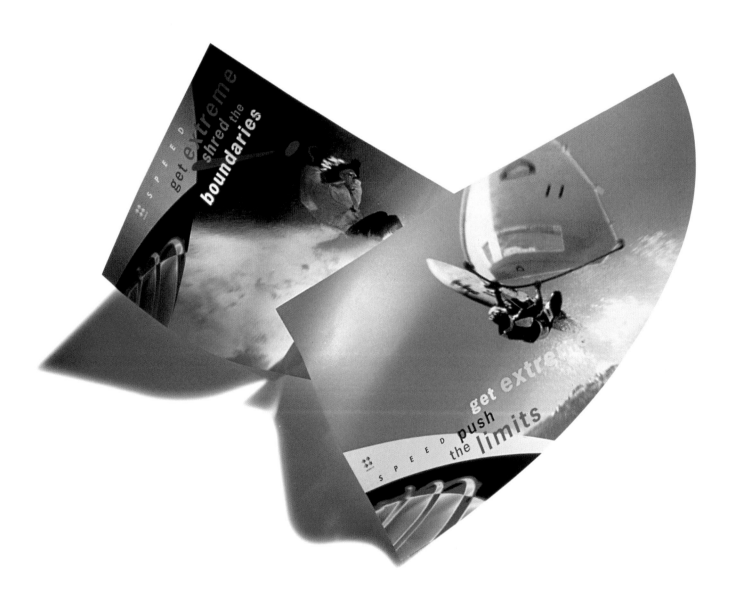

Design Firm: Carmichael Lynch
Thorburn
Creative Director: Bill Thorburn
Designer: Chad Hagen
Photographer: Bill Phelps
Copywriter: Jonathan Sunshine
Client: Minneapolis Association
of Children's Health Care

(opposite)
Design Firm: Pentagram Design
Art Director: Paula Scher
Designers: Paula Scher, Lisa Mazur,
Anke Stohlman
Photographer: Lois Greenfield
Client: Ballet-Tech

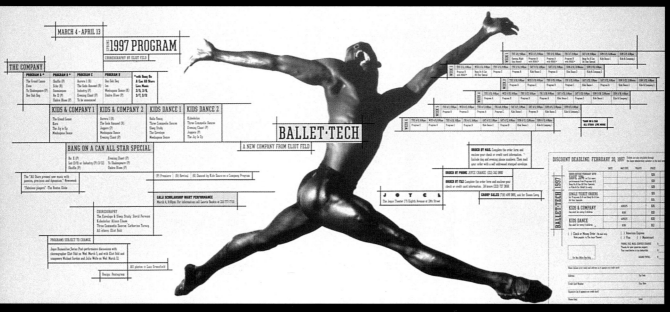

Design Firm: Hornall Anderson Design Works
Art Director: Jack Anderson
Designers: Jack Anderson,
Lisa Cerveny, Jana Wilson
Client: Best Cellars

Design Firm: Morla Design
Creative Director, Copywriter: Brian Collins
Art Director: Jennifer Morla
Designers: Jennifer Morla, Ann Culbertson,
Gaby Brink
Photographer: Cesar Rubio
Client: Foote, Cone, & Belding/Levi Strauss & Co.

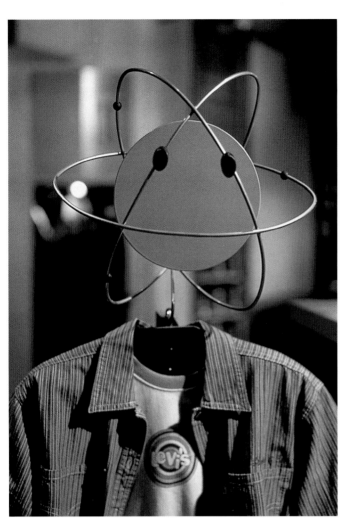

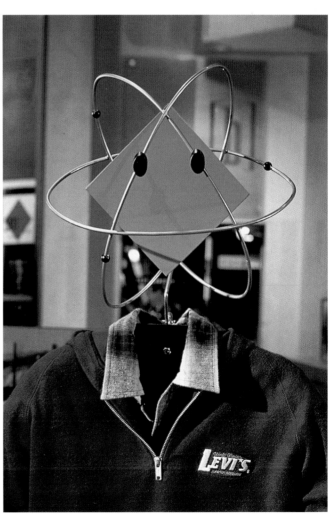

Designer: Jaap Drupsteen
Client: The Bank of the Netherlands

(opposite)
Design Firm: Illustration
Art Directors: Stefan Reiche,
McCann-Erickson GmbH
Illustrator: Peter Krämer
Client: U.S. Airways

THE LITTLE
GAME
ENGINE
THAT COULD.
NOW SMALLER – AND
MORE COLORFUL. AND
STILL THE LEADER IN
PORTABLE GAMING.

**U.S.
MARKET SHARE**

JANUARY – APRIL 1997

GAME BOY	86%
SEGA GAME GEAR	9%
NOMAD	5%

**WORLDWIDE
INSTALLED BASE**

UNITS IN MILLIONS	—— WORLDWIDE	···· U.S./CANADA

60
55
30
20
1989 (DATE OF LAUNCH) — APRIL 1997

**WORLDWIDE
SOFTWARE SALES**

UNITS IN MILLIONS	—— WORLDWIDE	···· U.S./CANADA

250
235
125
80
1989 (DATE OF LAUNCH) — APRIL 1997

SOURCE: TRSTS UNADJUSTED DATA
AND NINTENDO RESEARCH

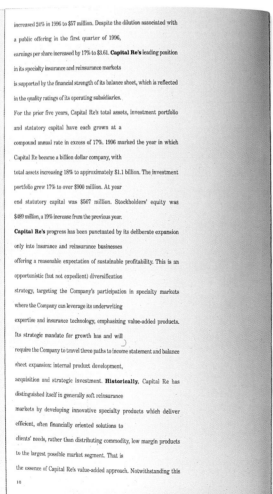

increased 24% in 1996 to $57 million. Despite the dilution associated with

a public offering in the first quarter of 1996,

earnings per share increased by 17% to $3.61. **Capital Re's** leading position

in its specialty insurance and reinsurance markets

is supported by the financial strength of its balance sheet, which is reflected

in the quality ratings of its operating subsidiaries.

For the prior five years, Capital Re's total assets, investment portfolio

and statutory capital have each grown at a

compound annual rate in excess of 17%. 1996 marked the year in which

Capital Re became a billion dollar company, with

total assets increasing 18% to approximately $1.1 billion. The investment

portfolio grew 17% to over $900 million. At year

end statutory capital was $567 million. Stockholders' equity was

$489 million, a 19% increase from the previous year.

Capital Re's progress has been punctuated by its deliberate expansion

only into insurance and reinsurance businesses

offering a reasonable expectation of sustainable profitability. This is an

opportunistic (but not expedient) diversification

strategy, targeting the Company's participation in specialty markets

where the Company can leverage its underwriting

expertise and insurance technology, emphasizing value-added products.

Its strategic mandate for growth has and will

require the Company to travel three paths to income statement and balance

sheet expansion: internal product development,

acquisition and strategic investment. **Historically,** Capital Re has

distinguished itself in generally soft reinsurance

markets by developing innovative specialty products which deliver

efficient, often financially oriented solutions to

clients' needs, rather than distributing commodity, low margin products

to the largest possible market segment. That is

the essence of Capital Re's value-added approach. Notwithstanding this

10

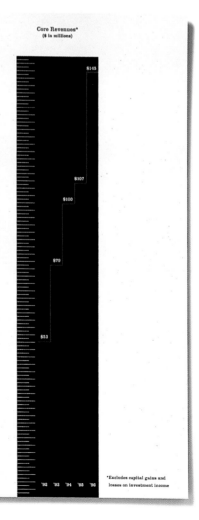

Core Revenues*
($ in millions)

$145
$107
$100
$79
$53

'92 '93 '94 '95 '96

*Excludes capital gains and
losses on investment income

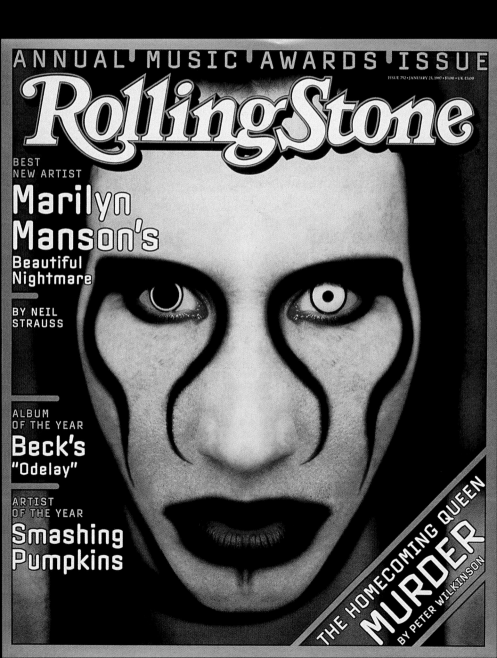

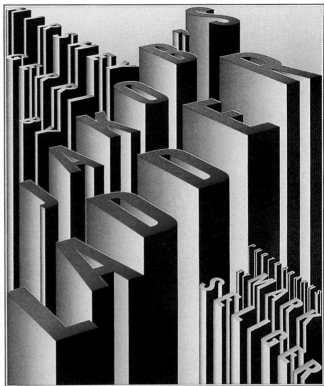

CHRIS ROCK STAR

BY FRED SCHRUERS PHOTOGRAPHS BY MARK SELIGER

BEING AMERICA'S FUNNIEST MAN IS NO SIMPLE CASE OF BLACK AND WHITE

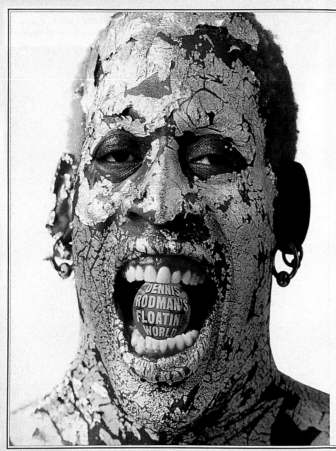

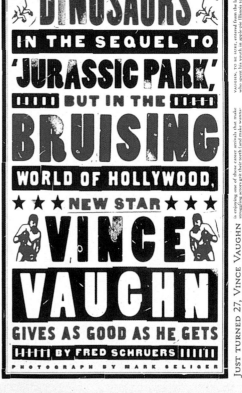

||| HE TAKES ON |||
DINOSAURS
IN THE SEQUEL TO
'JURASSIC PARK,'
BUT IN THE
BRUISING
WORLD OF HOLLYWOOD,
★ ★ ★ NEW STAR ★ ★ ★
VINCE
VAUGHN
GIVES AS GOOD AS HE GETS
||||| BY FRED SCHRUERS |||||
PHOTOGRAPH BY MARK SELIGER

JUST TURNED 27, VINCE VAUGHN is gripping one of those career arrivals that make he's get on the next Greyhound from Kansas to Hollywood. As the martini-sipping, skirt-chasing Trent in Jon Favreau's *Swingers*, Vaughn used a refrain that fit him like a lounge lizard's suit: "You are so money, baby."

LEGENDS OF COUNTRY MUSIC

PORTFOLIO BY MARK SELIGER

· 168 ·

Johnny Cash

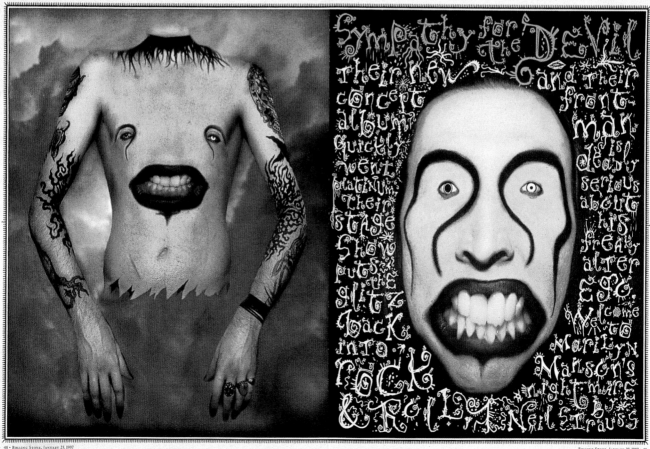

Sympathy for the DEVIL their new concept album quickly went platinum. Their stage show puts the glitz back into ROCK & ROLL and their frontman is deadly serious about his freaky alter ego. Welcome to Marilyn Manson's nightmare by Neil Strauss

Photographer: Eric Tucker (bottom right)
Illustrator: Tony Klassen (bottom left)
Copywriters: Kevin Kelly, Gary Wolf
Client: Wired

an infinite number of ingenious ways.

Media abhors a vacuum. It will colonize any vacant communication channel. And advertising – a type of communication – will follow. Media will also fill any possible means of communication, from pokey single-bit transmissions to industrial-strength mind melds. The communications revolution we initiated a decade ago continues to grow new habitats for media settlement. The largest so far is the low-bandwidth, still largely phone-based Internet, with some early hints of the high-band future to come. All we can say is, Let a thousand media types bloom. Soon.

Because as rapid as the arrival of networked pull media was, the second act – networked push media – is coming even faster. The Web took everyone (digerati included) by surprise; a new media materialized in the cavities of the phone system over the space of a few months. Push media will surprise again, quietly arriving under our noses, disguised as screensavers and pager messages and new channels on old Web sites.

At the risk of repeating ourselves, the technology and social forces that make a networked push revolution likely can be reduced to this:

There are other less lethal uncertainties. Like all new power, network media can cut both ways. The distinguishing characteristic of the new push media is that it finds you, rather than you finding it. That means the content knows where you are and what you are seeing. When you connect to a Castanet channel and receive a Java applet, you also have a bot that knows your address. When ActiveX lands on your hard drive, you have an active stranger in your box. This is good news and bad news. The good news is that push technology increases relationships, which by definition are two-way. Information flows back up and across. But the threat to your privacy and your tranquility is hard to miss: the more media smartifacts know about you, the better they work. What is not clear is how each new variation of push-pull, ambient, ultimate media will extract their costs. If these new media follow the pattern of other new technologies before them (and nothing we know about them indicates otherwise), the near future will see a cycle of extension and unification. Some will extend the capabilities of the old; we have PointCast extending the Web into push. Some will unify these new capabilities; we have the new Intercast chip from Intel unifying the Web with TV. Extension

Media is a tool – tools are media.

new tool, and wouldn't know how to use it if they did. Umberto Eco

Page 144

1) Increasingly fat data pipes and increasingly big disposable displays render more of the world habitable for media.
2) Advertisers and content sellers are very willing to underwrite this.
3) The ever-expanding network model that started with the postal system and telephones is being transplanted to this new ecology.
4) Do-it-yourself is great, but as in most aspects of life, people prefer ready-made. And when it comes to information, that means getting things from trusted sources.

Taken together, these certainties suggest we'll see a new media upswell that will make the remarkable phenomenon of 150 million Web pages created in 24 months seem slow and mild.

One large uncertainty remains. Currently in the US, networked media are mostly granted full freedom of speech. Radiated media, on the other hand, are regulated. And push content, carried by "scarce" radiated spectrum – TV – is fiercely regulated. If governments should be so stupid as to regulate the new networked push media as they have the existing push media, the expansion of media habitat could falter.

Written by Kevin Kelly and Gary Wolf,

with contributions from other Wired staff: Erik Adigard, Andrew Anker, Ed Anuff, John Battelle, Chip Bayers, John Browning, Jim Daly, Pete Leyden, Hunter Madsen, Oliver Morton, Spencer Reiss, Louis Rossetto, and Carl Steadman.

creates sexy new stuff, which is great but also complicated, creating opportunities for unification, to resupply warm, familiar fuzzy convenience. Extend, unify, extend further.

Each cycle of extend/unify notches up the ratchet of media complexity. Ontogeny recapitulates phylogeny, in interactive media as in biological life. All new media – including networked media – recapitulate the evolution of former media, until the new media eventually achieve their own limits. So online media have evolved from smoke signals (email) to books and magazines (the Web). We are now about to arrive at television (push media), before we finally emerge into what interactivity is really about. This next stage is at once immersive, engaging, responsive, pervasive, and always on. Smooch your cranky old browser one last time, because it's going bye-bye.

We think we "surf" the Web now, but what we really do is hopscotch across fragile stepping-stones of texts, or worse, spelunk in a vast unmapped cave of documents. Only when waves of media begin to cascade behind our screens – huge swells of unbrowsable stuff – will we truly surf.

The First Posthuman Talent Agency

Michael Rosenblatt, Ivan Gulas – founders, Mirage Entertainment Sciences

Considering all the struggling actors in Hollywood, it's no wonder that the first talent agency for synthespians is causing the latest Glittertown buzz. Ever since Michael Rosenblatt, cofounder of Atlantic Entertainment Group, and Harvard clinical psychologist Ivan Gulas (from left below) founded Mirage Entertainment Sciences in Boston last January, the active marketing of computer-generated actors has moved from idea to reality. There first brainchild is a blond and buxom beauty named Justine (right), modeled after the wife of scientist and artist-in-residence Mark Sagar. Gulas, who specializes in the correlation between human emotions and expression, brought Justine to life with a CAD system called Life F/x. The program, which grows out of software used to re-create human cells for medical imaging, adds a new level of photorealism to animation. "We're even able to wrinkle skin so it behaves like real tissue," Gulas says. With such fine detail, it's understandable that human actors fear a digital Demi Moore might one day push them off the screen. But Rosenblatt insists that he's not in the business of replacing actors. "We're just expanding the repertoire of creativity," he says. "After all, why do we have Mickey Mouse instead of a guy dressed up in a mouse suit?"
– Rachel Lehmann-Haupt

Stereo Is Dead, Long Live Internet Audio

Elizabeth Cohen – president, Audio Engineering Society

Face it: your last experience with "CD-quality" audio on the Internet was reminiscent of listening to an old AM radio. That burns up Elizabeth Cohen, a tireless crusader to improve the sound of audio online. "Music is in the transportation business," says Cohen. "But unless we get the audio issues sorted out, the Internet is never going to deliver an immersive entertainment experience." Her task is to galvanize disparate forces – from slick music execs to techies and entertainment providers – and get them moving in the same direction. She seems uniquely qualified for the job. Cohen is a PhD who is as comfortable discussing acoustic transmission protocols as she is raving about the percussive intricacies of the Grateful Dead. Her task is to enhance, from start to finish, the quality of audio delivery. She's pushing an agenda that includes the emergence of advanced Internet backbones for broadband sound transmission (she's a big fan of Internet2), the move to six-channel discrete audio ("stereo is dead," she says definitively), and the creation of electronic payment schemes for audio-based applications. "We must rally to get the quality of audio we need and, frankly, deserve." Sound advice.
– James Daly

Rent Movies on the Web

Stuart Skorman – founder, Reel.com

As the king of the East Coast's Empire video chain, Stuart Skorman became famous for movie-matching – a crude paper system that linked a list of films to his customers' preferences. Today Skorman, 48, is pushing movie-matching into cyberspace.

Through his Web site (www.reel.com), you can not only get movies delivered to your door, but also access an online system called Reel Genius that asks you to rate flicks from one to ten, then builds a customer profile. Skorman admits he's a sucker for action movies, but Reel.com is aimed at the art-film crowd. His store in Berkeley, California, stocks 35,000 rental titles and has more than 80,000 titles for sale. "Most video stores are centered around products – we're centered around information," he says. Seven-day rentals start at US$3 plus $6 postage; films arrive in two to three business days (overnight is also an option). Skorman says that as the next five to ten years technology will allow film fans to download movies instantly, directly into their TV or PC screens. And you can bet Reel.com will be one of the first video on-demand outlets at the starting gate.
– Rachel Lehmann-Haupt

(this page; opposite top, middle)
Design Firm: Life (in-house)
Art Director, Designer: Tom Bentkowski
Photographer: Gregory Heisler
Photo Editor: Alison Morley
Client: Life

(opposite, bottom)
Design Firm: Socio X
Art Director: Bridget de Socio
Designer: Lara Harris
Photographer: Nina Schultz
Copywriter: Christine Muhlke
Client: Paper Magazine

■ MOST OF HIS FRIENDS ARE DEAD ■ THOSE WHO POSED FOR HIM ARE GONE ■ HIS OWN BODY IS BEGINNING TO FALTER ■ BUT AS HE NEARS 80, AMERICA'S MOST BELOVED ARTIST IS WORKING WITH MORE CLARITY AND FEROCITY THAN EVER ■

Wyeth

By George Howe Colt
Photography by Harry Benson

HEAVY THINKING 1666

GRAVITY HELPED EXPLAIN THE HEAVENS—AND HOW HUMANS STAY DOWN TO EARTH.

UP the RIVER

Styled by Sleenen Storm | Makeup by Sarah
Hoover | Hair by Mateo Nico/Maria Niox NY
Models: Bernadette/Click, Crystal/IMG,
Eric Damon/DNA, Giuggolo Cecilino, Barton
Jahncke, Maria Niox, Speedy/DNA, Chris
Stevens/Company | Photographer's assistant:
Barton Jahncke | Stylist's assistant: Liz Oreding,
Makeup artist's assistant: Giampaolo Cantino

(this page;
opposite, left to right from top, 1–3, 5–8)
Design Firm: Socio X
Art Director: Bridget de Socio
Designers: Lara Harris, Albert Lin,
Jason Endres, Ninja V. Oertzen
Photographers: Nina Schultz (this page),
Massimo Capodieci (1),
Diego Uchitel (2), Mike Ruiz (3, 6),
Mark Lyon (4),
Norma Zuniga (5),
Jean-Pierre Khazem (7)
Copywriter: Christine Muhlke
Client: Paper Magazine

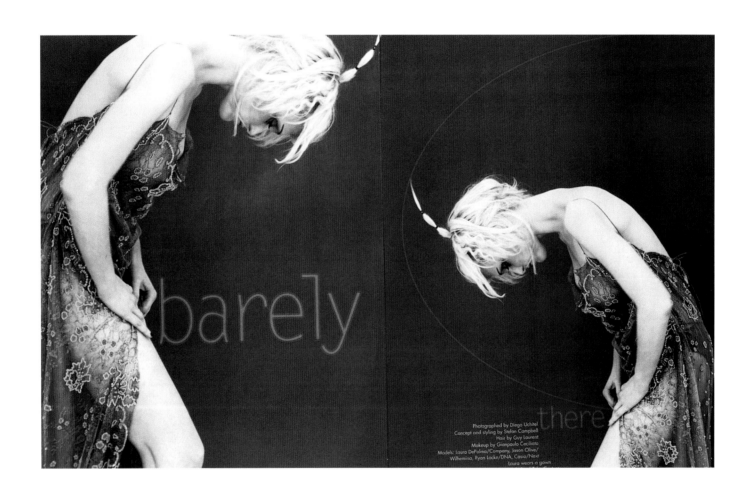

barely there

Photographed by Diego Uchitel
Concept and styling by Stefan Campbell
Hair by Guy Laurent
Makeup by Gianpaulo Ceciliato
Models: Laura DePalma/Company, Jason Olive/
Wilhemina, Ryan Locke/DNA, Casio/Next
Laura wears a gown

(opposite, 4)
Design Firm: Socio X
Art Director: Bridget de Socio
Designer: Ninja V. Oertzen
Photographer: Mark Lyon
Client: Fashion Reporter

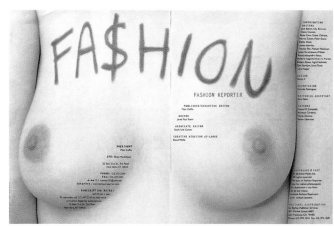

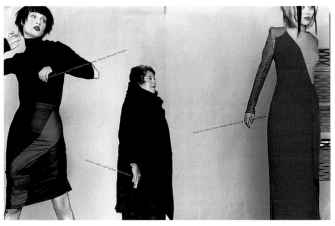

1 2
3 4
5 6
7 8

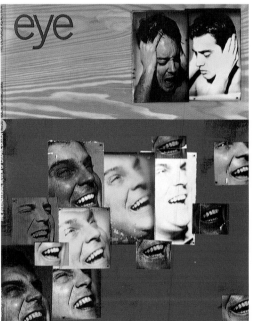

(top, bottom)
Design Firm: Pentagram Design
Creative Director: Lowell Williams
Art Directors: Lowell Williams, Bill Carson
Designers: Bill Carson, Marc Stephens
Client: USAA Foundation

(middle)
Design Firm: Eye (in-house)
Art Director: Stephen Coates
Photography: Anthony Oliver
Client: Quantum Publishing

(opposite)
Design Firm: Fantagraphics Books (in-house)
Creative Director, Art Director, Designer:
Monte Beauchamp
Client: Fantagraphics Books

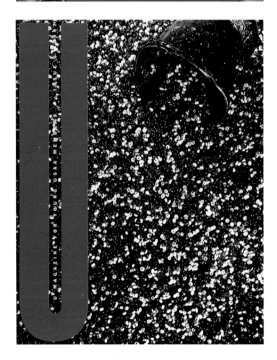

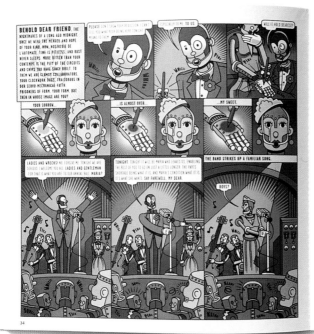

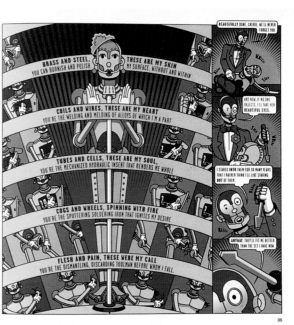

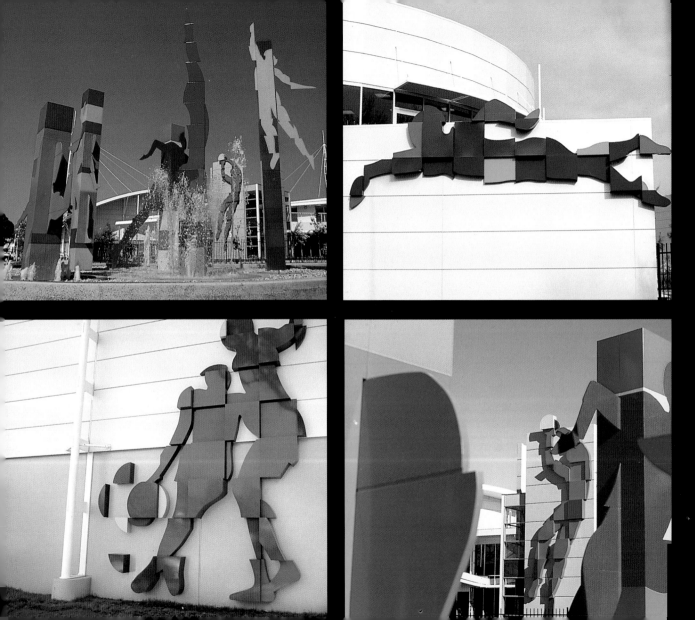

Design Firm: Pentagram Design
Art Director: Woody Pirtle
Designers: Woody Pirtle, Tracey Cameron,
Karen Parolek
Client: Fujisankei Communications Group

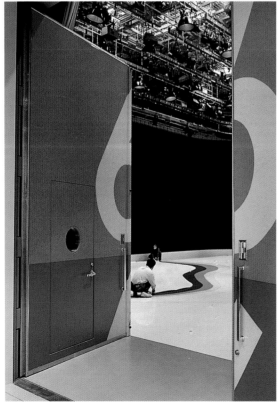

Design Firm: The Leonhardt Group
with Corbin Design
Designers: Mark Popich, Robert Brengman
Client: REI

Design Firm: Pentagram Design
Art Director: Paula Scher
Designers: Paula Scher, Anke Stohlman
Client: The Public Theater

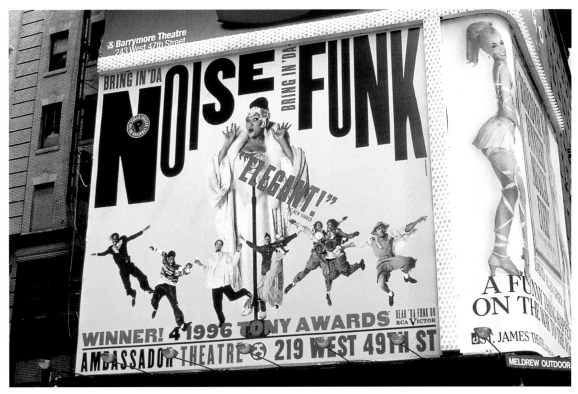

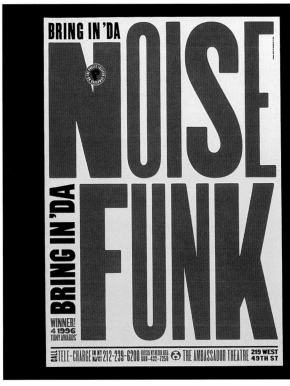

Design Firm: T L Horton Design, Inc.
Creative Director, Art Director, Designer:
Tony L. Horton
Photographer: Joe Aker
Client: Zap at Stratosphere

Design Firm: Addis Group
Art Director: Rick Atwood
Designers: Rick Atwood, Joanne Hom,
James Eli, Scott Bevan, Dale Hoover
Client: Ghirardelli Square

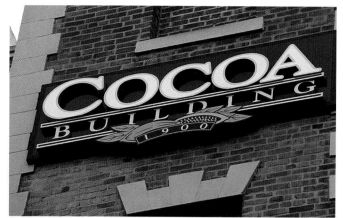

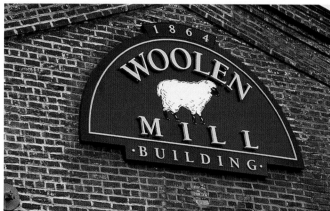

Art Director: John Clark
Designer: John Clark, Donna Fischer
Illsutrator: Brian Graham
Client: Martin Brattrud

(opposite, bottom)
Design Firm: Gee + Chung Design
Art Director, Designer: Earl Gee
Photographer: Andy Caulfield
Client: Visible Interactive

(this page)
Design Firm: Looking
Art Director: John Clark
Designers: John Clark,
Marianne Thompson
Client: MTV Networks

Design Firm: Elixir Design
Art Director: Jennifer Jerde
Designer: Jennifer Huff-Breeze
Client: Elixir Design

(opposite)
Design Firm: R2 Art, Inc.
Creative Director: Brian Murphy
Art Director: Renee Renfrow
Client: Adidas

Design Firm: R2 Art, Inc.
Creative Director: Brian Murphy
Art Director: Renee Renfrow
Client: Adidas

(opposite)
Design Firm: McGaughy Design (in-house)
Creative Director, Art Director, Designer:
Malcolm McGaughy
Client: McGaughy Design

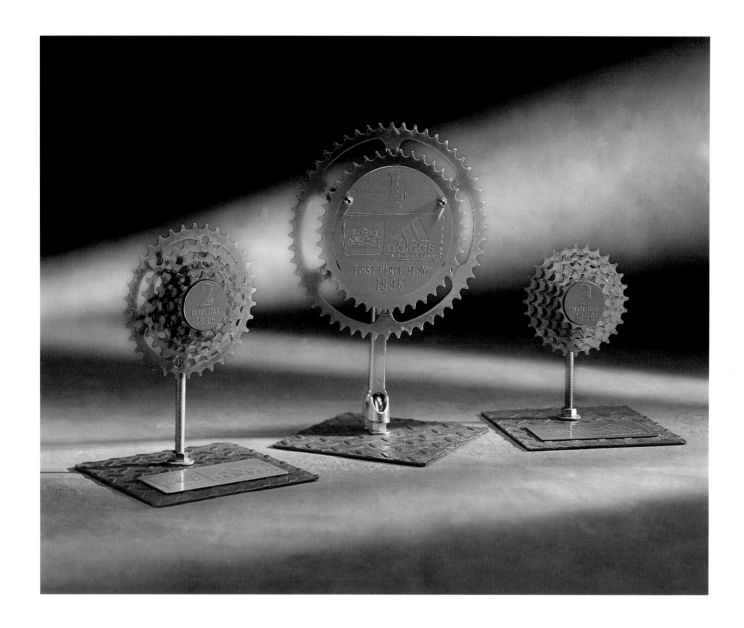

carrying out or going through a particular series of actions. **4.** the course or lapse, as of time. **5.** *Biol.* a natural outgrowth or projecting part. **6.** *Law.* a court action or summons. —*v.t.* **7.** to treat or prepare by some particular process, as in manufacturing. **8.** to handle in a routine, orderly manner.

pro·ces·sion (prə sesh′ən), *n.* **1.** a line or group of persons or things moving along in an orderly way, as in a parade. **2.** any continuous movement forward.

pro·ces·sion·al (prə sesh′ə nªl), *n.* a hymn suitable for accompanying a religious procession. —**pro·ces′sion·al·ly,** *adv.*

proc·es·sor (pros′es ər), *n.* **1.** Also, **proc′ess·er.** a person or thing that processes. **2.** the device within a computer that handles data. **3.** See **food processor.**

pro·claim (prō klām′, prə-), *v.t.* to announce formally or publicly. — **pro·claim′er,** *n.* —**proc·la·ma·tion** (prok′lə mā′shən), *n.*

pro·cliv·i·ty (prō kliv′i tē), *n., pl.* -ties. a strong habitual inclination or tendency, esp. toward something bad.

pro·con·sul (prō kon′səl), *n.* **1.** a governor or military commander of a province in ancient Rome. **2.** any administrator over a dependency or an occupied area. —**pro·con′su·lar,** *adj.* —**pro·con′su·late,** *n.* —**pro·con′sul·ship′,** *n.*

pro·cras·ti·nate (prō kras′tə nāt′, prə-), *v.i., v.t.,* -nat·ed, -nat·ing. to put off (action) habitually till another day or time. (commonly seen with graphic designers who "habitually put off" doing their self-promotional holiday greetings until it's too late.)

pro·cre·ate (prō′krē āt′), *v.t., v.i.,* -at·ed, -at·ing. to beget or bring forth (offspring). —**pro′cre·a′tion,** *n.* —

Pro·crus·te·an (prō krus′tē ən), *adj.* (*often l.c.*) tending to produce conformity by violent or arbitrary means.

proc·tol·o·gy (prok tol′ə jē), *n.* the branch of medicine dealing with the rectum and anus. —**proc′to·log′ic** (-t°loj′ik), **proc′to·log′i·cal,** *adj.* — **proc·tol′o·gist,** *n.*

proc·tor (prok′tər), *n.* a university official who supervises students during examinations. —**proc·to′ri·al** (-tôr′ē əl, -tôr′-), *adj.*

proc·to·scope (prok′tə skōp′), *n.* an instrument for visual examination of the interior of the rectum. —**proc·to-**

scop·ic (prok′tə skop′ik), *adj.* — **proc·tos·co·py** (prok tos′kə pē), *n.*

proc·u·ra·tor (prok′yə rā′tər), *n.* (in ancient Rome) an imperial official with fiscal or administrative powers.

pro·cure (prō kyŏŏr′), *v.t.,* -cured, -cur·ing. **1.** to obtain by effort. **2.** to cause to occur. **3.** to obtain (women) for the purpose of prostitution. —**pro·cur′a·ble,** *adj.* —**pro·cure′ment,** *n.* —**pro·cur′er,** *n.* — **pro·cur′ess,** *n.fem.*

prod (prod), *v.,* prod·ded, prod·ding, *n.* —*v.t.* **1.** to poke or jab with something pointed. **2.** to rouse to do something. —*n.* **3.** a poke or jab. **4.** any pointed instrument for prodding, as a goad.

prod., **1.** produce. **2.** produced. **3.** producer. **4.** product. **5.** production.

prod·i·gal (prod′ə gəl), *adj.* **1.** wastefully extravagant. **2.** lavishly abundant. —*n.* **3.** a person who is wastefully extravagant. —**prod′i·gal′i·ty** (-gal′i tē), *n.* —**prod′i·gal·ly,** *adv.* —**Syn. 1.** profligate. **2.** bountiful, profuse.

pro·di·gious (prə dij′əs), *adj.* **1.** extraordinary in size or amount. **2.** wonderful or marvelous: *a prodigious feat.* —**pro·di′gious·ly,** *adv.* — **pro·di′gious·ness,** *n.*

pro·duce (*v.* prə dōōs′, -dyōōs′; *n.* prod′ōōs, -yōōs, prō′dōōs, -dyōōs), *v.,* -duced, -duc·ing, *n.* —*v.t.* **1.** to bring into existence by labor, machine, or thought. **2.** to bring forth or yield. **3.** to present or show for inspection. **4.** to cause or give rise to. **5.** to get (a play, motion picture, etc.) organized for public presentation. —*v.i.* **6.** to bring forth or yield something. —*n.* **7.** something produced, esp. vegetables and fruits. —**pro·duc′er,** *n.* —**pro·duc′i·ble,** *adj.*

prod·uct (prod′əkt, -ukt), *n.* **1.** a thing produced, as by labor. **2.** a result or outcome. **3.** *Math.* the result obtained by multiplying two or more quantities together.

pro·duc·tion (prə duk′shən), *n.* **1.** the act of producing. **2.** product (def. 1). **3.** an amount that is produced. **4.** the organization and presentation of a dramatic entertainment. —**pro·duc′tive,** *adj.* —**pro·duc′tive·ly,** *adv.* — **pro·duc·tiv·i·ty**

Mc·Gaug·hy De·sign (mə ga′ hē · di zīn′) wishes **1.** you **2.** your family, a joyous and safe holiday season—*and a happy new year!*

pro·em (prō′əm), *n.* an introductory discourse.

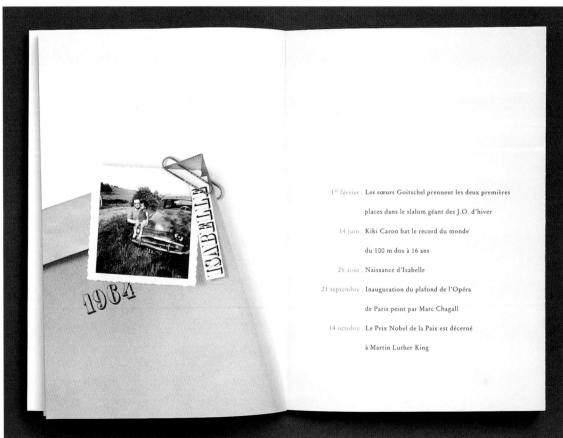

1ᵉʳ février . Les sœurs Goitschel prennent les deux premières
places dans le slalom géant des J.O. d'hiver

14 juin . Kiki Caron bat le record du monde
du 100 m dos à 16 ans

26 août . Naissance d'Isabelle

21 septembre . Inauguration du plafond de l'Opéra
de Paris peint par Marc Chagall

14 octobre . Le Prix Nobel de la Paix est décerné
à Martin Luther King

(opposite)
Design Firm: Le Petit Didier
Client: Isabelli & Bernard Schmitt

(this page)
Design Firm: John Brady Design Consultants, Inc.
Art Director: John Brady
Designer: Jim Bolander
Copywriter: Emily Ricketts
Client: International Sports Marketing

(this and following spread)
Design Firm: Pentagram Design
Client: San Jose Museum of Art
Art Director, Creative Director:
Kit Hinrichs
Designer: Hizam Haron

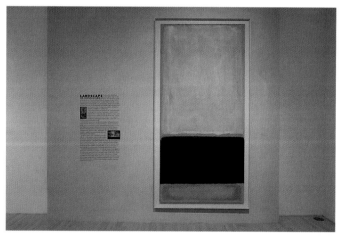

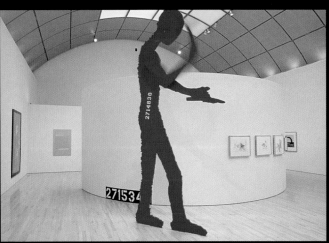

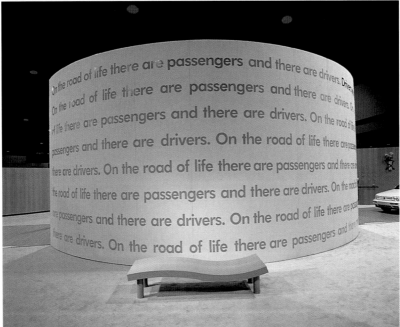

(opposite)
Design Firm: Mauk Design
Creative Director: Mitchell Mauk
Designers: Adam Brodsley,
Larry Raines
Photographer: Andy Caulfield
Client: Volkswagen of America

Design Firm: Hornall Anderson
Design Works, Inc.
Art Director: Jack Anderson
Designers: Jack Anderson, Jana Nishi, Heidi
Favour, David Bates, Sonja Max
Illustrator: Denise Weir
Copywriter: Suky Hutton
Client: Resource Games

LADY ARGENT

Art Director, Illustrator: Sandra Hendler
Client: Sandra Hendler, Inc.

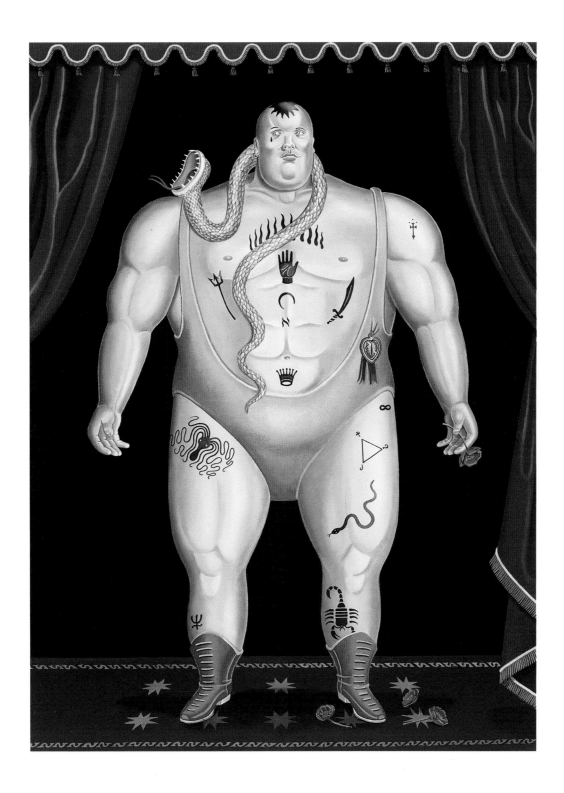

Design Firm: Illustration
Art Director: Paul Edison
Illustrator: Peter Krämer
Client: Smith Industries

(opposite)
Design Firm: Illustration
Art Director:
Alberto Garcia-Izquierdo
Illustrator: Peter Krämer
Editor: Peter Pletchacher
Client: Deutsche Lufthansa AG

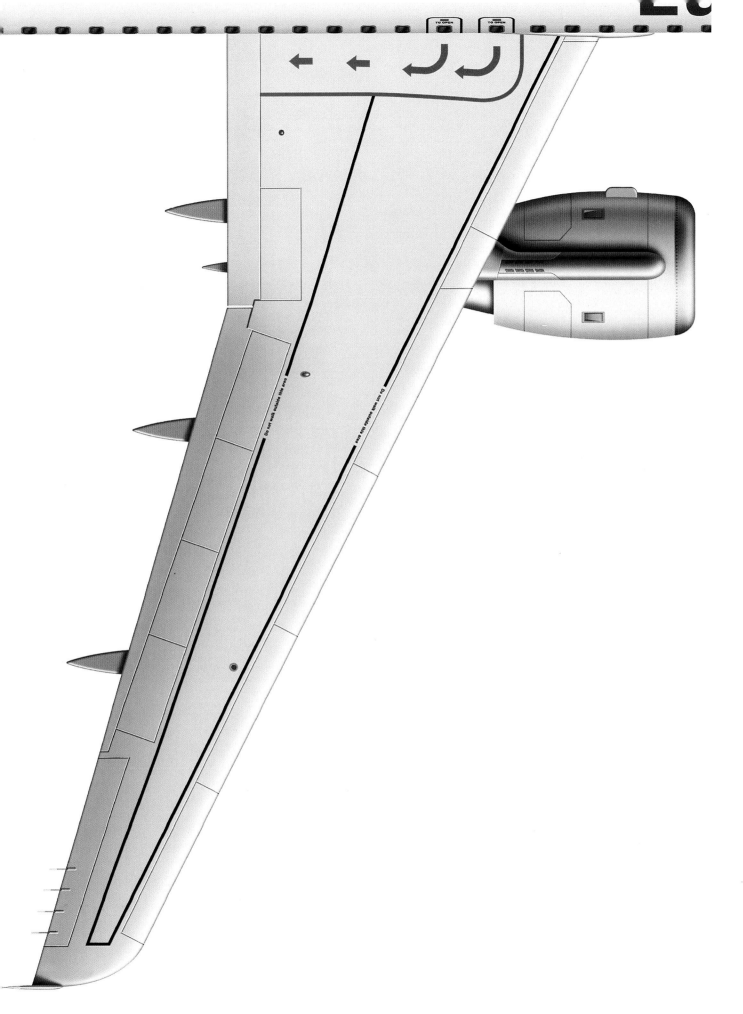

(opposite)
Design Firm: Bantam Doubleday
Dell (in-house)
Art Director: Jim Plumeri
Illustrator: Cathleen Toelke
Client: Bantam Doubleday Dell

(this page)
Design Firm: Henry Holt (in-house)
Art Director: John Candell
Illustrator: Cathleen Toelke
Client: Henry Holt

Design Firm: Ryan Drossman & Partners (in-house)
Client: Ryan Drossman & Partners
Creative Director: Neil Drossman
Designers: Richard Wilde, Roswitha Rodrigues
Illustrator: Martucci & Griesback

Design Firm: Origin Design Ltd. (in house)
Client: Origin Design
Art Directors: Blake Enting/Robert Achten
Designer: Blake Enting
Illustrator: Watermark

Design Firm: Drive Communications (in-house)
Art Director, Designer: Michael Graziolo
Photographer: Michael Watson
Client: Drive Communications

Design Firm: Carmichael Lynch Thorburn (in-house)
Creative Director: Bill Thorburn
Designer: Chad Hagen
Illustrators: Chad Hagen, David Schrimpf
Client: Carmichael Lynch Thorburn

(top)
Design Firm:
Pfeiffer plus Company
Art Director, Designer:
Todd Doyle
Client: Reprox Printing

(bottom)
Design Firm: Imagination
Corporation (in-house)
Art Director, Designer:
Heather Gomes
Illustrator: Lesley Brink
Client:
Imagination Corporation

Design Firm:
Deep Design
Art Director, Designer:
Rick Grimsley
Client:
Litho-Krome Company

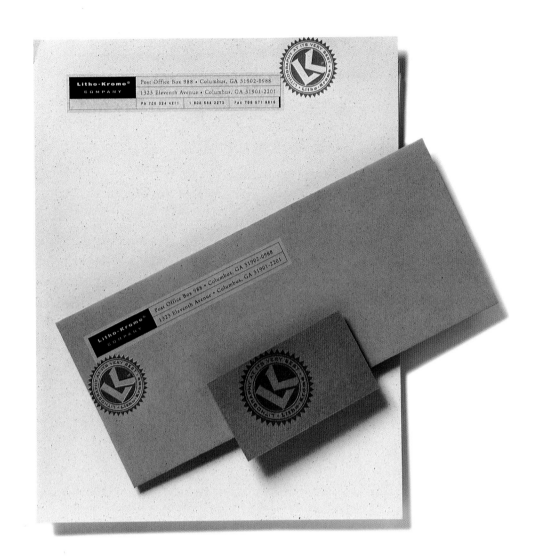

Design Firm:
Sargent & Berman
Art Director, Designer:
Peter Sargent
Illustrator:
Bill Ticineto
Client:
Tool Box Productions

Design Firm: Ambrosini Design
Creative Director: Ken Ambrosini
Designers: Anne Koenig Snider,
Ken Ambrosini
Client: Ambrosini Design

(opposite, top)
Design Firm: Alternativ Studio
Art Director, Designer: Péter Vajda
Photographer: András Láng-Miticzky
Client: Aedificium

(opposite, middle)
Design Firm: GSD&M Advertising
Creative Director: Cindy Clevenger
Designer: Brett Stiles
Illustrator: Mike Griswald
Client: Cigar Lounge

(opposite, bottom)
Design Firm: Mullen Advertising
Art Director, Designer: Ginger Hood
Illustrator: Coco Masuda
Client: Osram Sylvania

Design Firm: Insight Design
Communications
Art Directors, Creative Directors,
Designers: Sherrie Holderman,
Tracy Holderman
Client: Fresh Paint

(opposite, left to right from top, 1)
Design Firm: Pentagram Design
Art Director, Designer: John Klotnia
Client: Micrus Corporation

(2) Design Firm: RBMM
Art Director, Designer, Illustrator:
Tom Nynas
Client: Heaven Connection

(3) Design Firm: Pennebaker.LMC
Creative Director: Jeffrey McKay
Art Director, Designer, Illustrator:
Greg Valdez
Client: Rathgeber/Talley

(4) Design Firm: Charles S. Anderson
Design Company
Art Directors: Charles S. Anderson,
Todd Piper-Hauswirth
Designer: Todd Piper-Hauswirth
Client: Winsor Sport Fencing

(5) Design Firm: Sibley/Peteet Design
Art Director, Designer: David Beck
Photographer: Sean McCormick
Client: Haggar Apparel Company

(6) Design Firm:
Charles S. Anderson Design Company
Client: Henry Engine Company
Art Director: Charles S. Anderson
Designer: Jason Schulte

(7) Design Firm: Joseph Rattan Design
Art Director, Designer:
Brandon Murphy
Illustrators: Brandon Murphy,
Diana McKnight
Client: Rainforest Shopping Center

(8) Design Firm: Brainstorm Inc.
Creative Director, Art Director,
Designer, Illustrator: Chuck Johnson
Client: Legacy Capitol Group

(9) Design Firm: Lewis
Advertising/Nashville
Art Director: Robert Froedge
Client: Nellie's Originals

Design Firm: Michael Osborne Design
Creative Director, Designer:
Michael Osborne
Client: San Francisco Museum
of Modern Art

(opposite, from top)
(1) Design Firm: Hatmaker
Creative Directors: Tom Corey,
Marianna Gracey
Art Director: Tom Corey
Designers: Haig Bedrossian, Tom Corey
Illustrator: Ted Smykal
Client: Universal Studios

(2) Design Firm: GSD&M Advertising
Designer, Illustrator: Patrick Nolan
Client: Texas Aerospace/1997 Paris
Airshow

©SFMOMA 1996

SAN FRANCISCO MUSEUM OF MODERN ART

(3) Design Firm: Thompson &
Company
Creative Director: Trace Hallowell
Art Directors: David Steinke,
Trace Hallowell
Designer: David Steinke
Client: Memphis AAA Baseball

(4) Design Firm: Tim Smith
Communication Design
Creative Director, Designer: Tim Smith
Client: AIGA/Cincinnati

(5) Design Firm: McDill Design
Art Director, Designer, Illustrator:
Joel Harmeling
Client: R.C. Schmidt

Design Firm: en Vision (in-house)
Art Director: Howell Hsiao
Designers: Vadim Goretsky, Lai-Kit Chan
Client: en Vision

(opposite)
Design Firm: Sackett Design Associates
Art Director, Creative Director:
Mark Sackett
Designers: Wayne Sakamoto,
James Sakamoto
Photographer: John Acuro
Client: Nightshade Restaurant

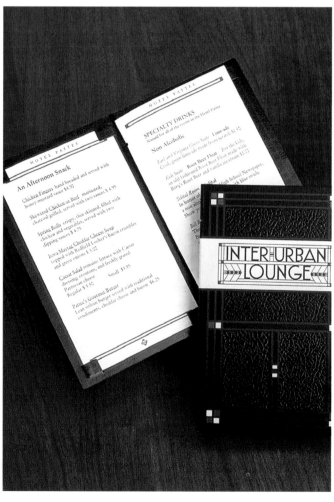

(opposite, top left, right)
Design Firm: Fitch
Art Director, Designer: Nick Richards
Copywiter: Jo French
Client: Amin Ali, The Red Fort

(opposite, bottom left)
Design Firm: Duffy Design
Creative Director: Joe Duffy

(opposite, top row)
Design Firm: Sagmeister Inc.
Art Director: Stefan Sagmeister
Designers: Stefan Sagmeister,
Hjalti Karlsson
Photographer: Tom Schierlitz
Copywriter: David Byrne
Model Creator: Yuji Yoshimoto
Client: Luaka Bop/Warner Bros.

(opposite, middle row)
Design Firm: Verve Records (in-house)
Art Director, Designer: Chika Azuma
Photographer: Barron Claiborne
Client: Verve Records

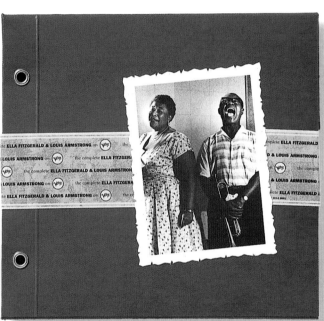

(opposite, bottom row)
Design Firm: Capitol Records (in-house)
Art Director, Designer: Jeff Fey
Photographer: Neal Preston
Client: Capitol Records

(left)
Design Firm: Capitol Records (in-house)
Creative Director: Tommy Steele
Art Director, Designer:
George Mimnaugh
Photographer: Glen Wexler
Client: Capitol Records

(right)
Design Firm: Verve Records (in-house)
Art Director, Designer: Giulio Turturro
Copywriter: William Ruhlman
Client: Verve Records

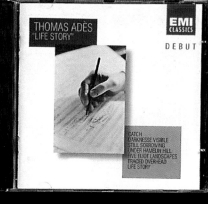

J.S. BACH
HARPSICHORD WORKS

EMI CLASSICS
DEBUT

RICHARD EGARR

ROSSINI
BELLINI
VERDI
DONIZETTI
WOLF-FERRARI
RESPIGHI

EMI CLASSICS
DEBUT

REBECCA EVANS
MICHAEL POLLOCK

THOMAS ADÈS
"LIFE STORY"

EMI CLASSICS
DEBUT

CATCH
DARKNESSE VISIBLE
STILL SORROWING
UNDER HAMELIN HILL
FIVE ELIOT LANDSCAPES
TRACED OVERHEAD
LIFE STORY

"STEAL AWAY"
SPIRITUALS & GOSPEL SONGS

EMI CLASSICS
DEBUT

RUBY PHILOGENE
LONDON ADVENTIST CHORALE
KEN BURTON · JULIUS DRAKE

PALESTRINA
MISSA ASSUMPTA EST MARIA
MAGNIFICAT SEPTIMI TONI
MOTETS

EMI CLASSICS
DEBUT

TIMOTHY BROWN

DUOS FOR
CLASSICAL ACCORDIONS
STRAVINSKY · MUSSORGSKY

EMI CLASSICS
DEBUT

JAMES CRABB
GEIR DRAUGSVOLL

CHOPIN
PIANO WORKS

EMI CLASSICS
DEBUT

NELSON GOERNER

PIANO TRANSCRIPTIONS OF WORKS BY
JOHANN STRAUSS II

EMI CLASSICS
DEBUT

KONSTANTIN SCHERBAKOV

MOZART
CLARINET QUINTET
FLUTE QUARTET NO.1
OBOE QUARTET

EMI CLASSICS
DEBUT

BRINDISI QUARTET
NICHOLAS CARPENTER
JAIME MARTIN
JONATHAN KELLY

(opposite, top)
Design Firm: Waste Mgt. Inc.
Creative Directors: Neil Kellerhouse, Hugh Brown
Art Director, Designer: Neil Kellerhouse
Photographer: Lee Tanner (cover),
Hugh Brown (interior sax photos)
Copywriters: Ira Gitler, Bob Porter
Client: Rhino Records

(opposite, bottom)
Design Firm:
Michele M. Humphrey Design
Art Director, Creative Director, Designer:
Michele M. Humphrey
Photographer: Marc Tule
Client: Mojave Sun Records

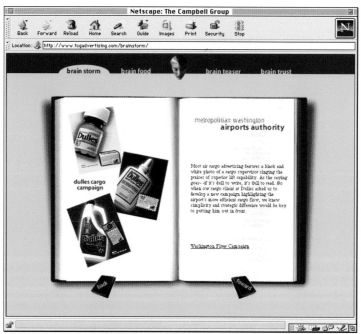

(opposite)
Design Firm: The Campbell
Group (in-house)
Creative Director: Andy Dumaine
Art Director: Mark Rosica
Photographer: Aaron Goodman
Copywriter: Andy Dumaine
Client: The Campbell Group

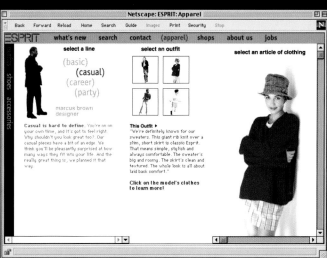

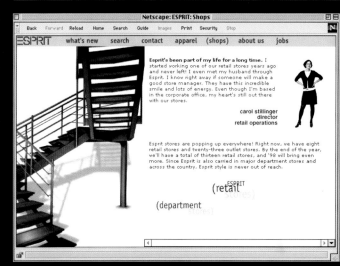

Design Firm: Adjacency
Creative Director: Andrew Sather
Art Director: Bernie DeChant

Design Firm:
Vigon/Ellis
Creative Director,
Art Director:
Larry Vigon
Designers:
Larry Vigon,
Brian Jackson
Client: Xiphias/
Encyclopedia Electronica
DVD Interface

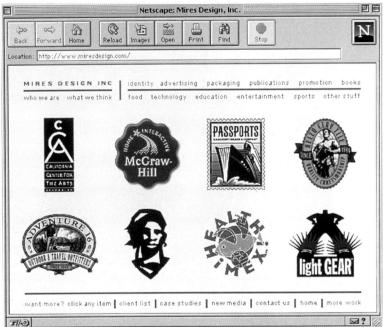

(opposite)
Design Firm: Mires Design
Client: (in-house)
Art Director: John Ball
Designers: John Ball, Jeff Samaripa,
Gale Spitzley
Copywriter: Brian Woolsey

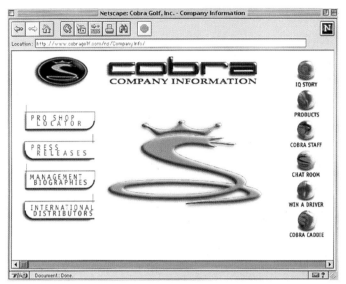

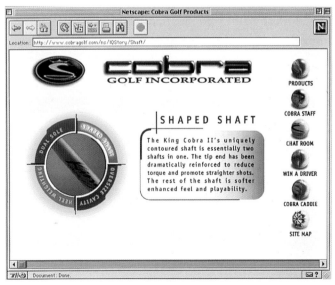

Design Firm: Mires Design
Art Director: José A. Serrano
Designers: Jeff Samaripa,
Eric Freedman, Kathy Carpentier-Moore
Client: Cobra Golf

Design Firm: Pentagram Design, Inc.
Art Director: Paula Scher
Designers: Paula Scher, Anke Stohlman
Client: The Public Theater

Design Firm: Pentagram Design, Inc.
Art Director, Designer: Woody Pirtle
Client: United Parcel Service

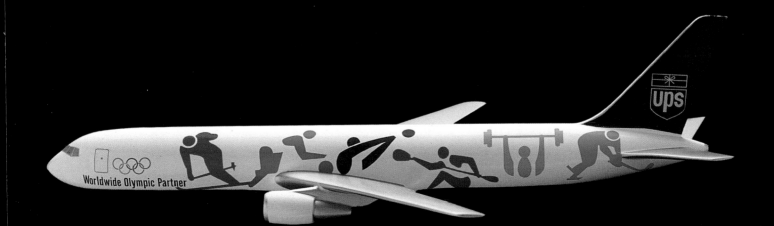

Design Firm: Mires Design
Art Director: José Serrano
Designers: José Serrano, Deborah Hom
Photographer: Carl Vanderschuit
Copywriter: Andrea May
Client: Qualcomm

(following spread, left page)
Design Firm: (in-house)
Creative Director: Carol Buettner Sherts
Art Director, Designer: Jane Church
Photographer: Richard Pierce
Client: Jon Frieda Professional Haircare

(following spread, right page)
Design Firm:
Desgrippes Gobe & Associates
Creative Director: Joel Desgrippes
Art Director: Sophie Fahri
Client: Celine

Design Firm: Butler, Shine & Stern
Creative Directors: Mike Shine, John Butler
Art Director, Designer: Luis Peña
Client: Hub Distributing/Millers Outpost

Design Firm: Nike, Inc. (in-house)
Creative Director: Ron Dumas
Art Director: Michele Melandri
Designers: Michele Melandri,
Steven Wittenbrook/SOMA
Photographer: David Emitte
Client: Nike, Inc.

(opposite)
Design Firm: Package Land Co. Ltd. (in-house)
Art Director, Designer: Yasuo Tanaka
Photographer: David Emitte
Client: Package Land Co. Ltd.

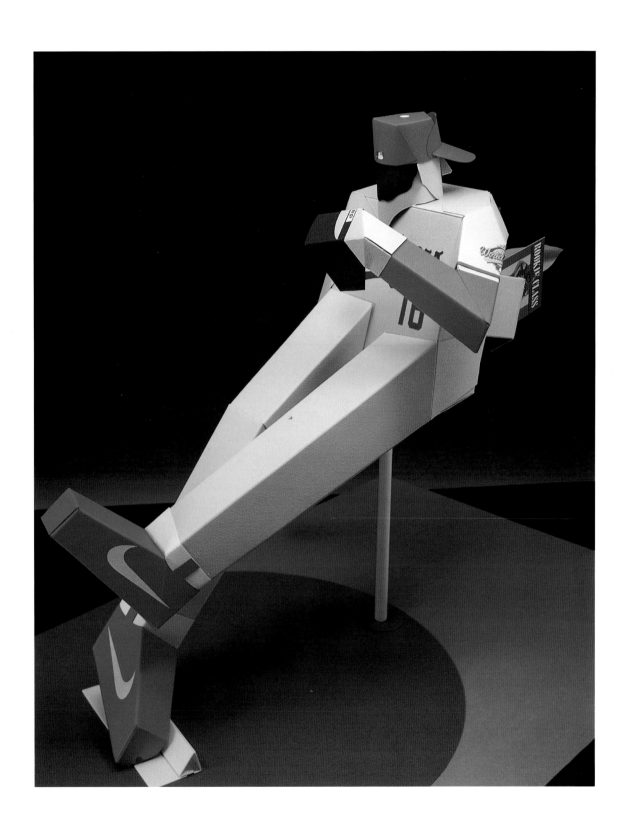

Design Firm: Romeo Empire Design Inc.
Creative Director, Designer:
Vincent Romeo
Photographer: Andy Shen
Client: Lizard Brand Cigars

(opposite)
Design Firm: Atelier Haase & Knels
Art Director, Illustrator: Sibylle Haase
Designers: Katja Hirschfelder,
Thomas Meyer, Thomas Paschke,
Judith Heinemann
Client: Sianwell Vertriess GmbH

Design Firm: Pennebaker.LMC
Creative Director, Art Director,
Designer: David Lerch
Client: McLellan Software Center

(opposite)
Design Firm: Fossil (in-house)
Creative Director,
Art Director: Tim Hale
Designer, Copywriter: John Dorcas
Client: Fossil

(opposite)
Design Firm: Pentagram Design
Creative Director, Art Director:
Kit Hinrichs
Designer: Garth Jordan
Client: Columbus Salame

(this page)
Design Firm: Carmichael Lynch
Thorburn (in-house)
Creative Director: Bill Thorburn
Art Director: Chad Hagen
Copywriter: Kathi Skow
Client: Carmichael Lynch Thorburn

(following spread, left page)
Design Firm: Compass Design
Creative Director: Mitchell Lindgren
Designers: Mitchell Lindgren, Tom Arthur, Rich McGowen
Illustrator: Tom Arthur
Client: Buckin' Bass Brewing Co.

(following spread, right page)
Design Firm: Parachute, Inc.
Creative Director: Jac Coverdale
Art Director, Designer: Heather Cooley
Illustrator: Mark Weakley
Photographer: Curtis Johnson
Copywriter: Jerry Fury
Client: Millennium Import. Co.

(opposite, top left)
Design Firm: Cato Design, Inc.
Photographer: Mark Rayner
Client: Peerick Vineyard

(opposite, top right, bottom)
Design Firm: Cato Design, Inc.
Photographer: Mark Rayner
Client: Turramurra Estate Vineyard

(this page, left)
Design Firm: Britton Design
Art Director, Designer: Patti Britton
Photographer: Mitch Rice
Illustrator: Evans & Brown
Client: Viansa Winery

(this page, right)
Design Firm: Britton Design
Art Director, Designer: Patti Britton
Photographer: Mitch Rice
Illustrator: Jay Palm Saddle Shop
Client: Galante Vineyards

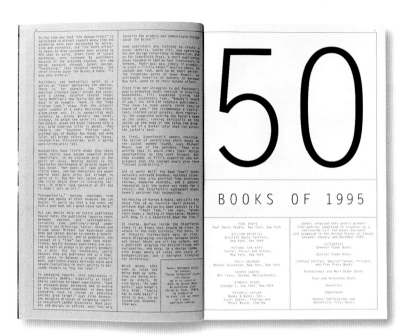

Design Firm: Pentagram Design
Art Director: Michael Bierut
Designers: Michael Bierut, Lisa Anderson
Client: Mohawk Paper Mills

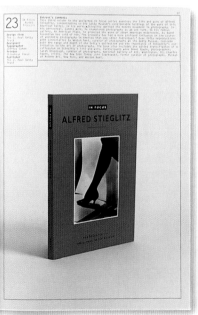

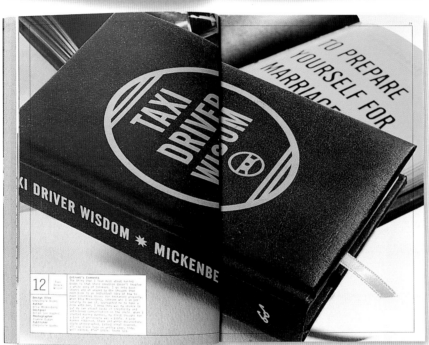

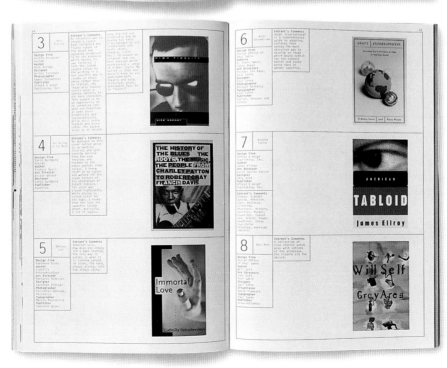

Design Firm:
Charles S. Anderson Design Company
Art Director: Charles S. Anderson
Designers: Jason Schulte, Todd Piper-Hauswirth
Photographers: Darrell Eager, Bill Phelps
Copywriter: Renee Valois
Client: French Paper Company

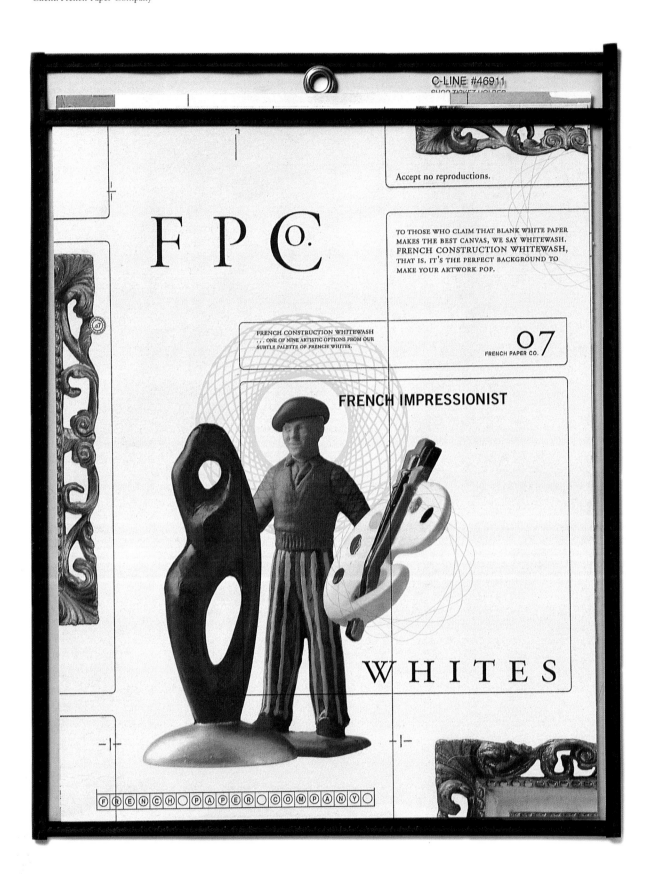

Design Firm: Studio d'Design
Art Director, Designer: Laurie Demartino
Photographer: Steve Belkowitz
Copywriter: Lisa Pemrick
Client: French Paper Company

Design Firm:
Charles S. Anderson Design Company
Art Director: Charles S. Anderson
Designer: Jason Schulte
Copywriter: Lisa Pemrick
Client: French Paper Company

(opposite)
Design Firm:
Cozzolino Ellet Design D'Vision
Creative Director, Art Director, Designer:
Phil Ellett
Photographer: Mike Rutherford
Client: Spicers Paper Limited

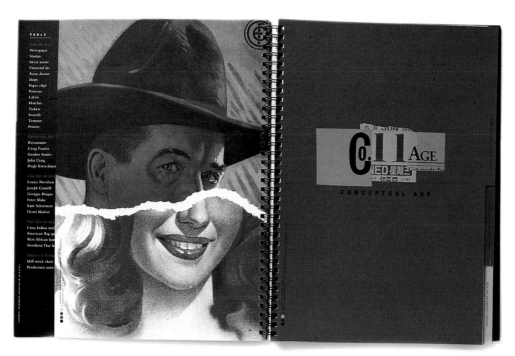

Co.11AGE

CONCEPTUAL ART

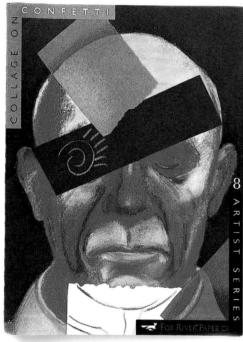

COLLAGE ON CONFETTI

8 ARTIST SERIES

FOX RIVER PAPER CO.

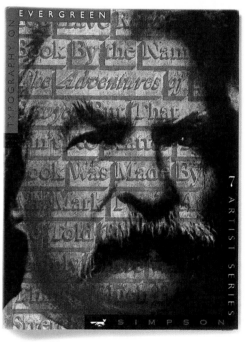

EVERGREEN

TYPOGRAPHY ON

Book By the Nam
The Adventures of

Book Was Made By
Mark

7 ARTIST SERIES

SIMPSON

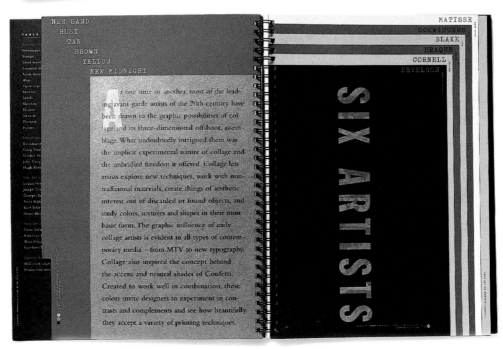

NEW SAND
RUST
TAN
BROWN
YELLOW
NEW MIDNIGHT

r one time or another, most of the leading avant-garde artists of the 20th century have
been drawn to the graphic possibilities of collage and its three-dimensional offshoot, assem-
blage. What undoubtedly intrigued them was
the implicit experimental nature of collage and
the unbridled freedom it offered. Collage lets
artists explore new techniques, work with non-
traditional materials, create things of aesthetic
interest out of discarded or found objects, and
study colors, textures and shapes in their most
basic form. The graphic influence of early
collage artists is evident in all types of contem-
porary media – from MTV to new typography.
Collage also inspired the concept behind
the accent and neutral shades of Confetti.
Created to work well in combination, these
colors invite designers to experiment in con-
trasts and complements and see how beautifully
they accept a variety of printing techniques.

MATISSE
SCHWITTERS
BLAKE
BRAQUE
CORNELL
NEVELSON

SIX ARTISTS

Warren Gloss 80Lb./118gsm

(opposite)
Design Firm: Pentagram Design
Creative Director, Art Director:
Kit Hinrichs
Designer: Amy Chan
Photographers: Bob Esparza,
Brian Mahany
Illustrator: Milton Glaser
Copywriter: Delphine Hirasuna
Client: Simpson/Fox River Paper

Design Firm: Siegel & Gale
Creative Director, Copywriter:
Cheryl Heller
Art Director: Veronica On
Client: S.D. Warren

Warren Gloss 80Lb./118gsm

Design Firm: Pennebaker.LMC
Creative Director: Jeffrey McKay
Art Directors: Greg Valdez,
Jeffrey McKay
Designer, Illustrator: Greg Valdez
Client: Lawndale Art
& Performance Center

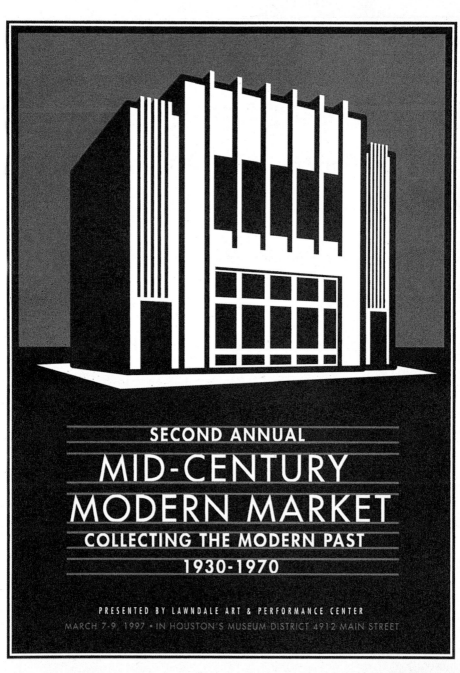

SECOND ANNUAL

MID-CENTURY
MODERN MARKET

COLLECTING THE MODERN PAST

1930-1970

PRESENTED BY LAWNDALE ART & PERFORMANCE CENTER

MARCH 7-9, 1997 ▪ IN HOUSTON'S MUSEUM DISTRICT 4912 MAIN STREET

SPONSORS: DAVID LACKEY ANTIQUES, MCCOY INC., MOOSE CAFE, PHYLLIS TUCKER ANTIQUES
DESIGN: PENNEBAKER.LMC   COORDINATION: PATRICIA R. SCHROEDER

(opposite)
Design Firm: Craig Frazier Studio
Creative Director, Art Director,
Designer, Illustrator: Craig Frazier
Client: AIGA/Colorado

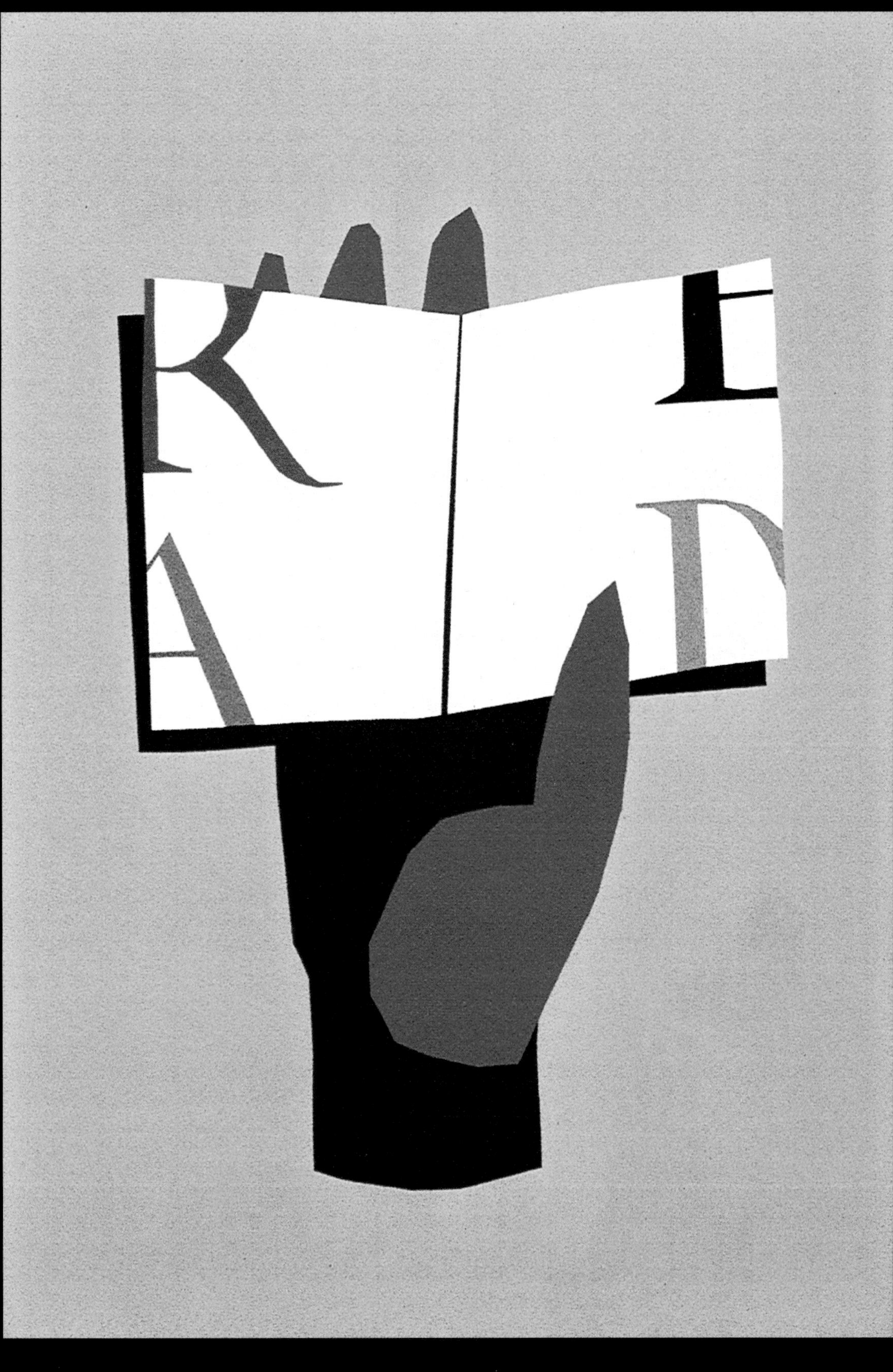

Design Firm:
Mires Design
Art Director:
Jose Serrano
Client:
Hot Rod Hell
Designer:
Jose Serrano, Jeff
Samaripa
Illustrator:
Tracy Sabin

(opposite)
Design Firm:
Carmichael Lynch
Thorburn
Creative Director:
Bill Thorburn
Designer:
Chad Hagen
Photographer:
Bill Phelps
Copywriter:
Jonathan Sunshine
Client:
Association
of Children's
Health Care

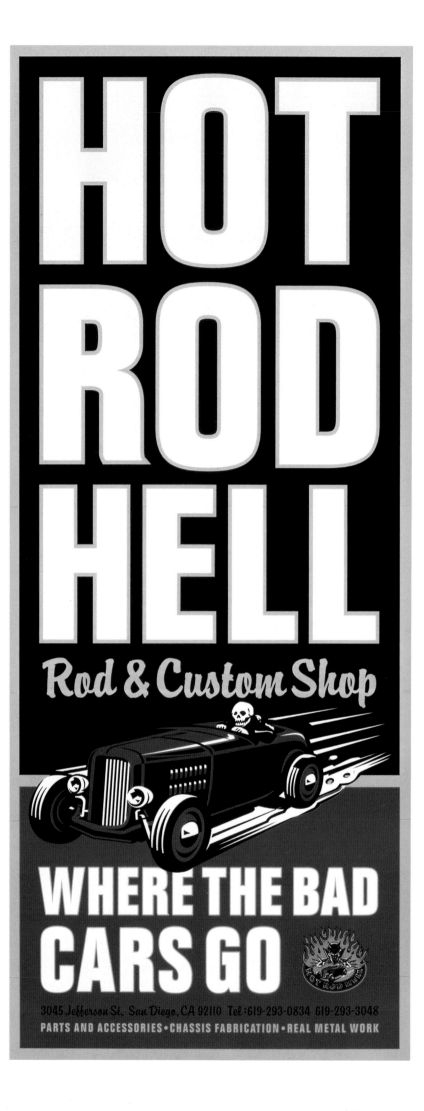

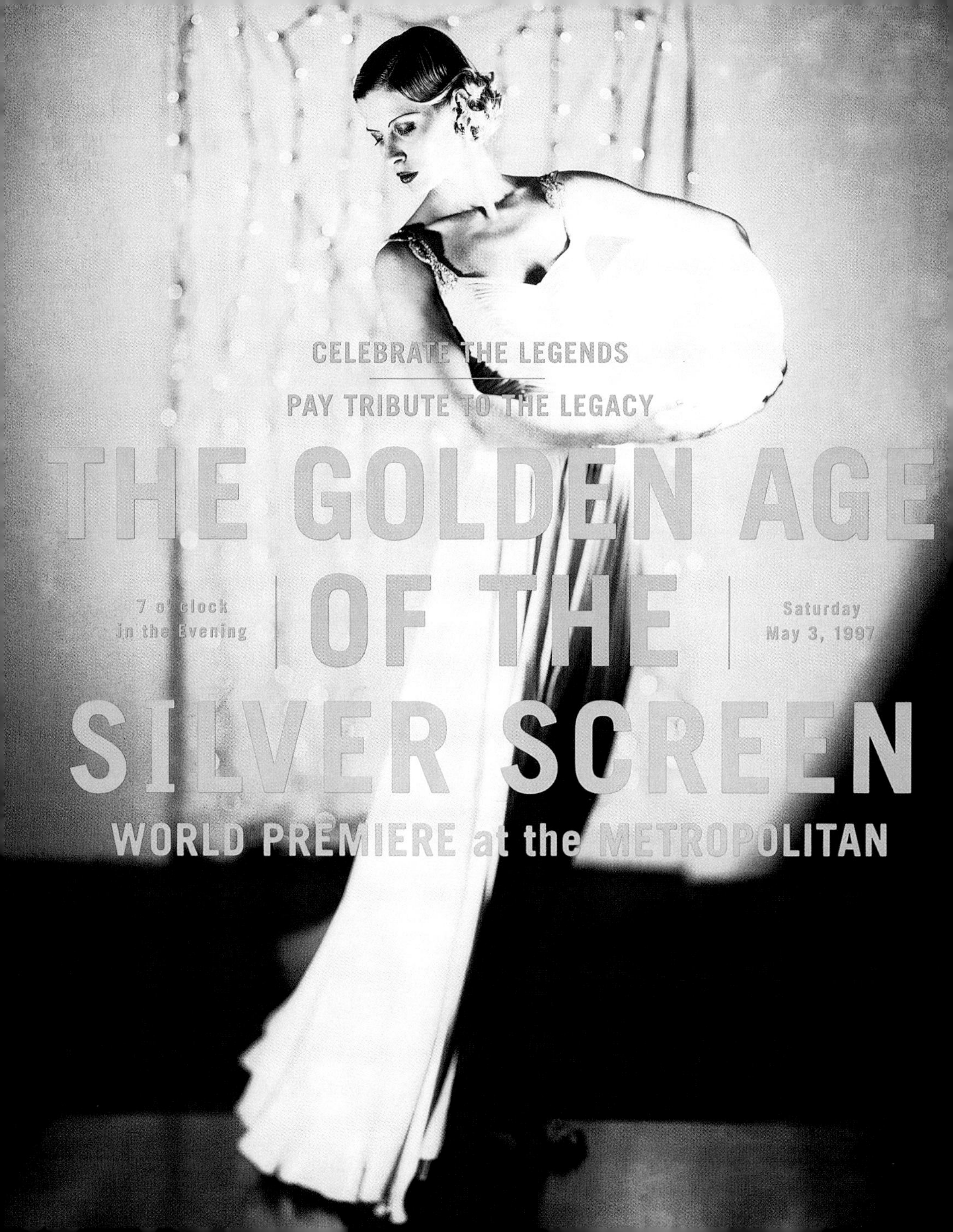

CELEBRATE THE LEGENDS

PAY TRIBUTE TO THE LEGACY

THE GOLDEN AGE
OF THE

7 o'clock
in the Evening

Saturday
May 3, 1997

SILVER SCREEN

WORLD PREMIERE at the METROPOLITAN

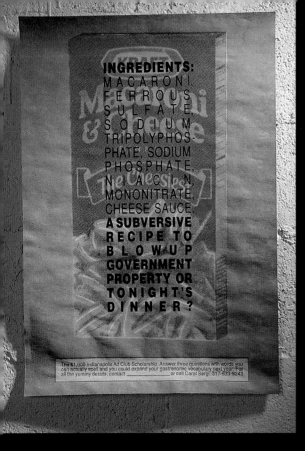

INGREDIENTS: MACARONI, FERROUS SULFATE, SODIUM TRIPOLYPHOS- PHATE, SODIUM PHOSPHATE, NIACIN, IRON, THIAMIN, MONONITRATE, CHEESE SAUCE. **A SUBVERSIVE RECIPE TO BLOW UP GOVERNMENT PROPERTY OR TONIGHT'S DINNER?**

The $1,000 Indianapolis Ad Club Scholarship. Answer three questions with words you can actually spell and you could expand your gastronomic vocabulary next year. For all the yummy details, contact _____ or call Carol Sergi, 317-633-9243.

INGREDIENTS: PORK PARTS, TURKEY PARTS, BEEF PARTS, FLAVORINGS. **HUNGER FOR KNOWLEDGE SHOULDN'T LEAD TO SWALLOWING A TURKEY BEAK.**

The $1,000 Indianapolis Ad Club Scholarship. Three questions are the only thing between you and eating higher off the hog next year. For the mouth watering details, contact _____ or call Carol Sergi, 317-633-9243.

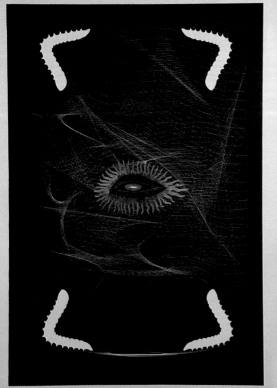

COMMUNI CATI ON

COMMUNI CATI ON

(opposite, top)
Design Firm: Young & Laramore Advertising
Creative Directors: David Young,
Jeff Laramore
Art Director: Chris Beatty
Designers: Scott Watanabe,
David Kirby Ballamy, Don Wheeler,
Kerry Foster, Tim Abare
Copywriter: Tim Abare
Client: Indianapolis Ad Club

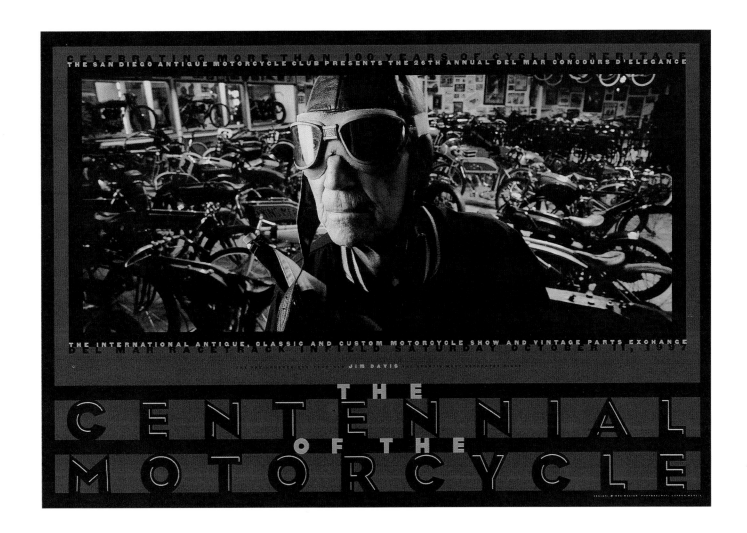

(opposite, bottom)
Design Firm: Shenzhen Xianjun
Design Co., Ltd. (in-house)
Art Director, Designer: Guo Xianjun
Client: Shenzhen Xianjun
Design Co., Ltd.

(this page)
Design Firm: Mires Design
Art Director: Scott Mires
Designers: Scott Mires, Eric Freedman
Photographer: Gordon Menzie
Client: The San Diego Antique
Motorcycle Club

Design Firm: Le Petit Didier
Illustrator: Jean Vodaine
Client: Médiatheque du Pontiffroy

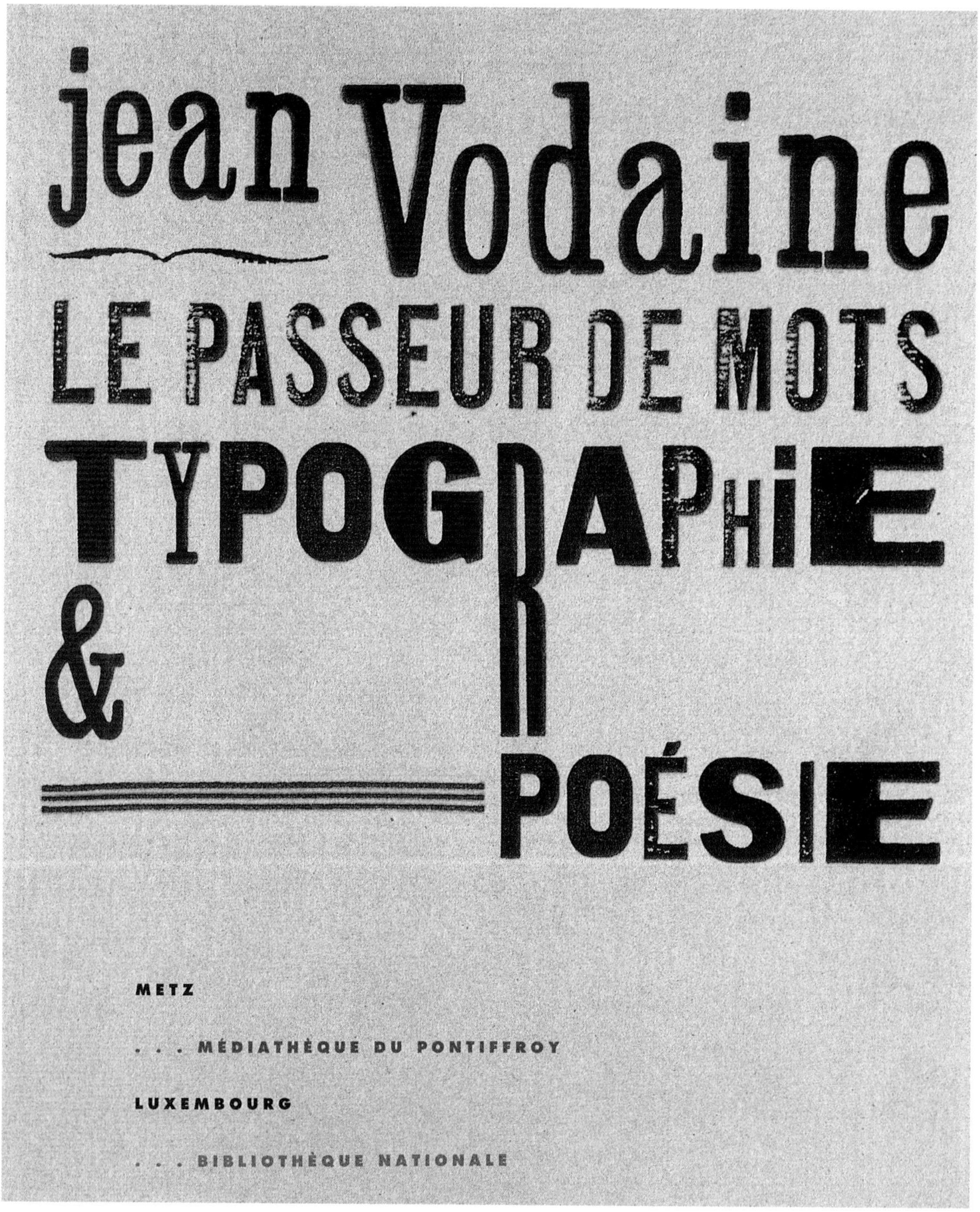

jean Vodaine
LE PASSEUR DE MOTS
TYPOGRAPHIE
& R
POÉSIE

METZ

. . . MÉDIATHÈQUE DU PONTIFFROY

LUXEMBOURG

. . . BIBLIOTHÈQUE NATIONALE

(opposite)
Design Firm: Gold-Grafik
Client: Erziehungsollreletion
d.Kt. Zurich

Einladung zum

SOMMERFEST

Freitag, 12. September

ab 18.00 Uhr

Lachen, trinken, tanzen... einfach so... plaudern...
sich amüsieren, die Gläser heben, den Gaumen
erfreuen, rauchen, lauschen, beschwipst sein und
beobachten, schmunzeln... immer weiter...
stundenlang, sich festsetzen, diskutieren, trällern,
Gesichter studieren, im Dunkeln munkeln,
Schummerlicht und Kerzenschein... genießen,
Häppchen ergattern... entspannen... der
Musik lauschen, pfeifen, träumen, versinken...
zurückkehren, erneut eintauchen, Schwätzchen halten,
schweigen, schunkeln, schnorren, sich zurücklehnen,
Grüppchen analysieren... und der Morgen erwacht,
einfach hinnehmen, der Wein mundet, die Zeit
ignorieren... "was soll's"... den Rhythmus fühlen,
Witze machen, lästern, Ringe blasen...
von Vorne beginnen...

Senefelderstrasse 18
70178 Stuttgart

Um Antwort wird gebeten!

Design Firm: Design Guys
Creative Director,
Art Director: Steven Sikora
Designer: Jay Theige
Photographer: Darrell Eager
Client: Theatre de la
Jeune Lune

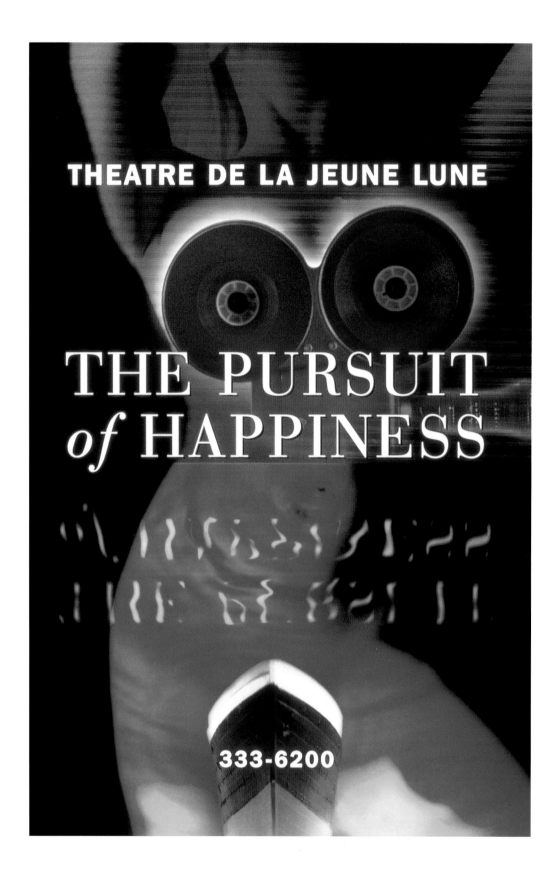

THEATRE DE LA JEUNE LUNE

THE PURSUIT
of HAPPINESS

333-6200

(opposite)
Design Firm: Cyclone
Designers, Illustrators:
Traci Daberko, Dennis Clouse
Photographer: Marco Prozzo
Client: Intiman Theatre

the TURN of the SCREW

ADAPTED BY JEFFREY HATCHER
HENRY JAMES' CLASSIC THRILLER
DIRECTED BY VICTOR PAPPAS
JULY 4TH THROUGH AUGUST 2ND
FOR TICKETS: 269-1900 OR 292-ARTS

INTIMAN
THEATRE
TWENTY-FIFTH SEASON
SPONSORED BY ERNST & YOUNG LLP
AND HARBOR PROPERTIES INC.

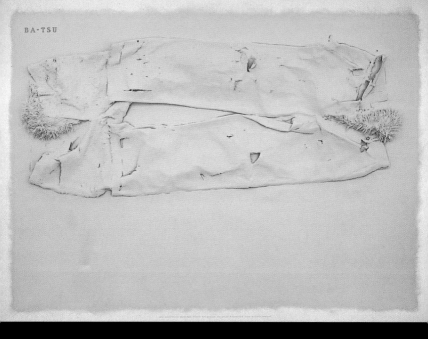

BA-TSU

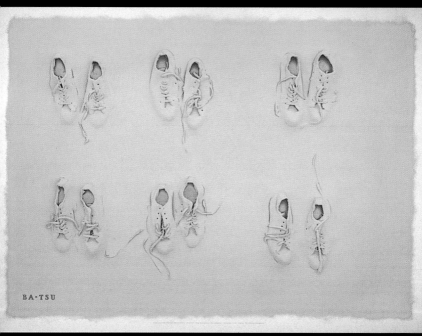

BA-TSU

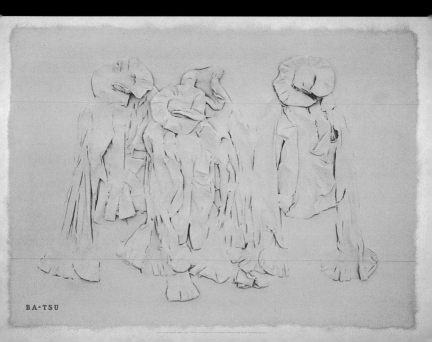

BA-TSU

(opposite)
Design Firm:
Makoto Saito Design
Client: Ba-tsu '97

(this page)
Design Firm:
Makoto Saito Design
Client: Masunaga

Design Firm: Zimmerman
Crowe Design
Art Director: Neal Zimmerman
Designer: Eric Heiman
Photographer: Everard Williams
Client: Levi Strauss & Co.

(opposite)
Design Firm: Nike, Inc. (in-house)
Creative Director: Ron Dumas
Art Director: Webb Blevins
Photographer: Peggy Sirota
Copywriter: Neil Webster
Client: Nike, Inc.

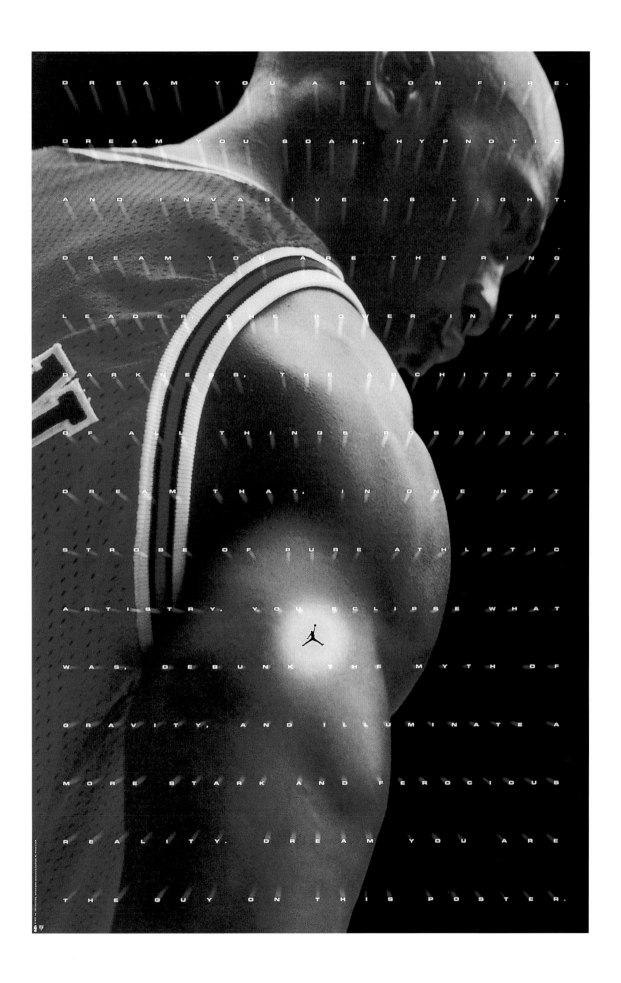

Design Firm: Nippon Design
Center, Inc.
Creative Director, Art Director,
Designer: Naoto Iwahashi
Client: Plans-eye Studio, Inc.

Design Firm: Packaging Create, Inc.
Development Organization
Art Director: Akio Okumura
Designer: Michiko Eguchi
Client: Osaka Bay Area

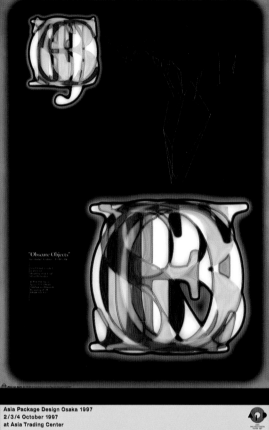

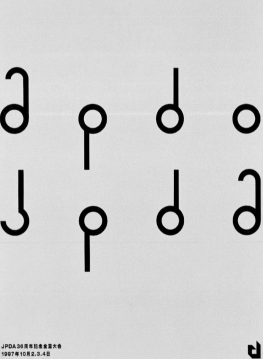

For
Nature
and
You

HEIWA PAPER

Design Firm: Packaging Create Inc.
Art Director, Photographer: Nob Fukuda
Designer: Akio Okumura
Client: Heiwa Paper Co., Ltd.

行也自在

(opposite)
Design Firm: Kan & Lau Design Consultants
Art Director, Designer:
Freeman Lau Siu Hong
Client: Regional Council, Hong Kong

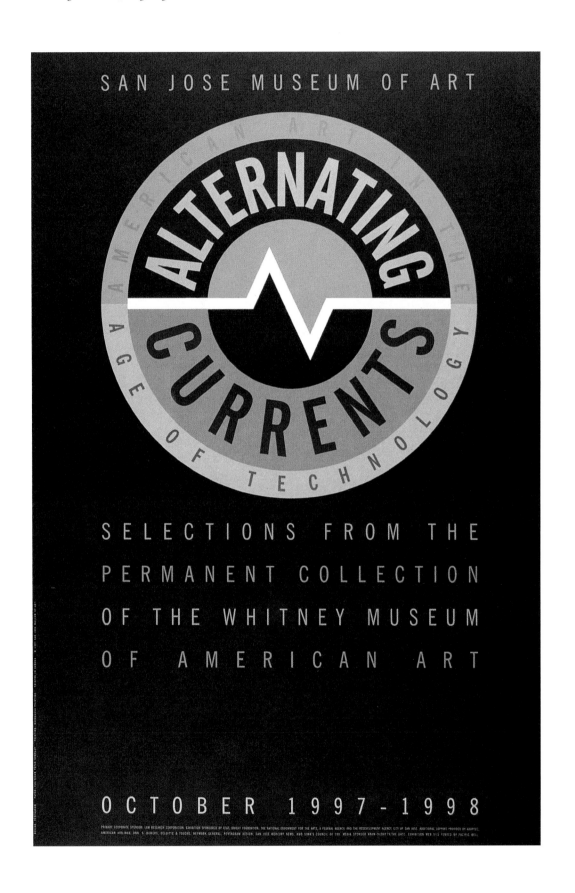

Design Firm: Pentagram Design
Designer: Hizam Haron
Creative Director, Art Director:
Kit Hinrichs
Client: San Jose Museum of Art

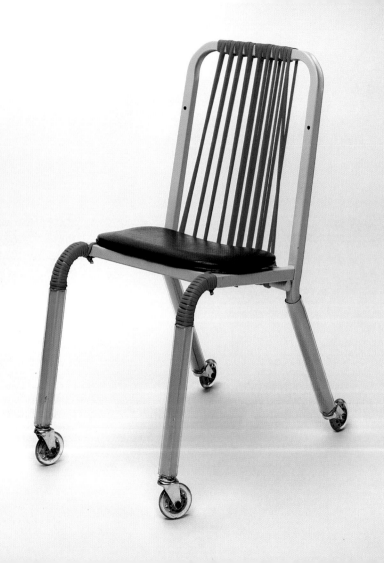

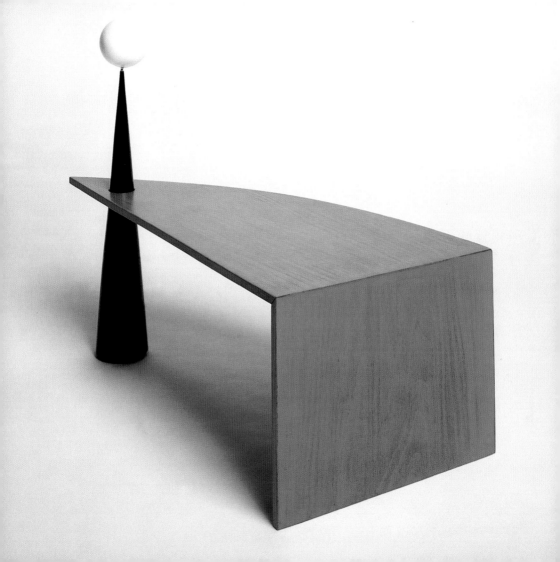

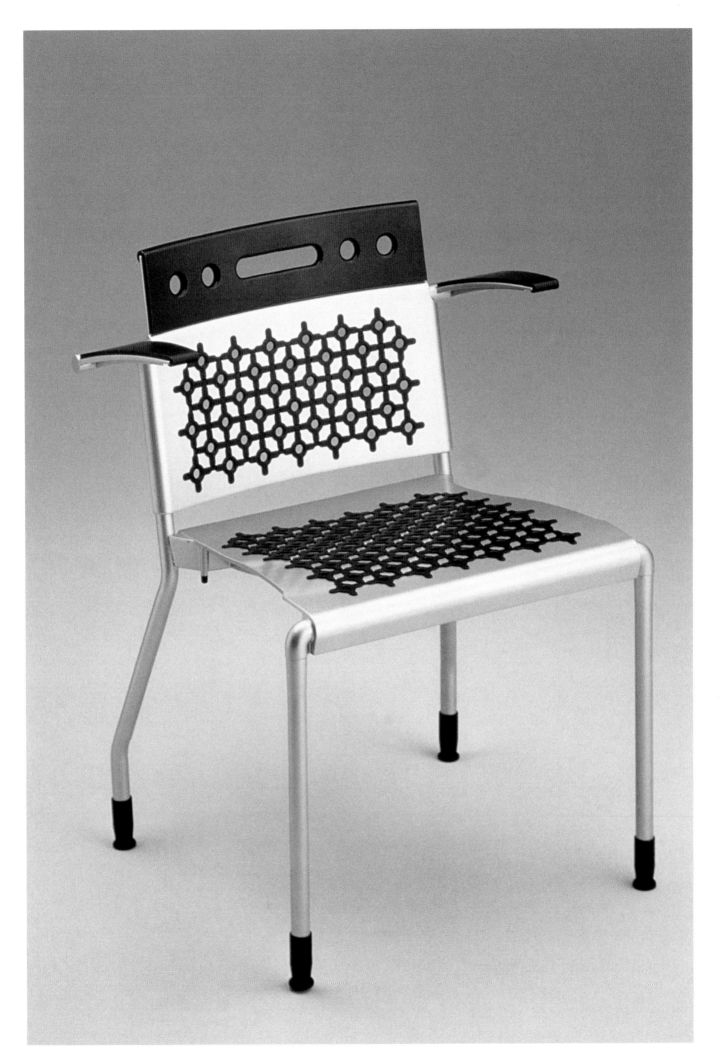

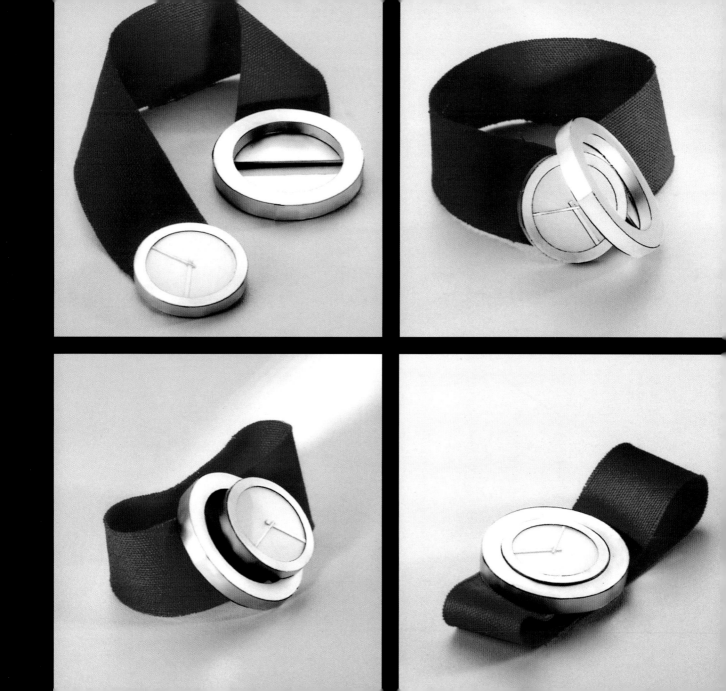

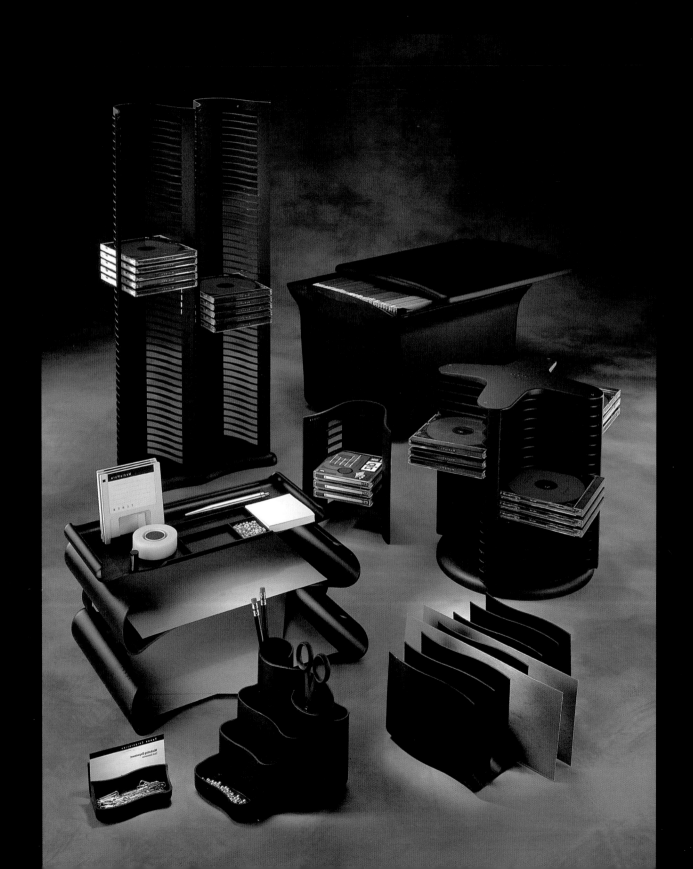

(opposite)
Design Firm: Herbst LaZar Bell, Inc.
Principle Designer: Mark Dziersk
Team Designers: Jose Perez,
Jon Lindholm, Sabrina Tongish
Photographer: Tom Petroff
Client: Tenex Filing Products

Design Firm: Kan & Lau
Design Consultants
Creative Director, Art Director,
Designer: Kan Tai-Keung
Client: Shiatos Ltd.

Design Firm: Danilo de Rossi
Designer: Danilo de Rossi
Client: Vetreria de Majo

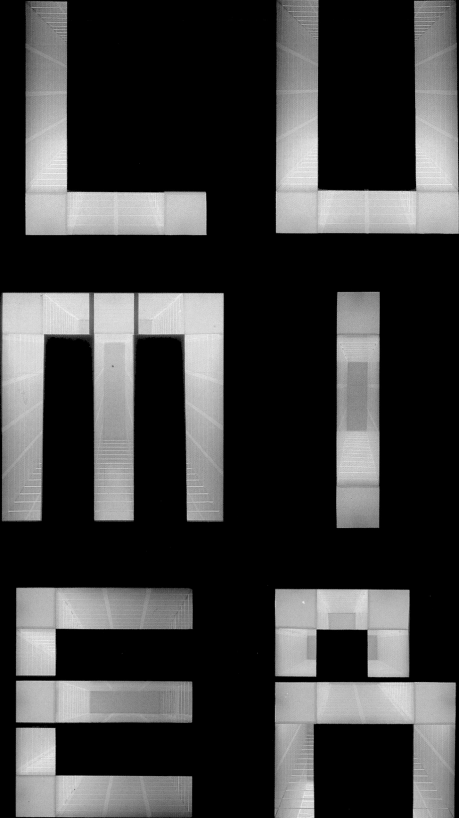

Design Firm: Shiseido Co., Ltd. (in-house)
Creative Director: Masao Ohta
Art Director, Designer: Aoshi Kudo
Client: Shiseido Co., Ltd.

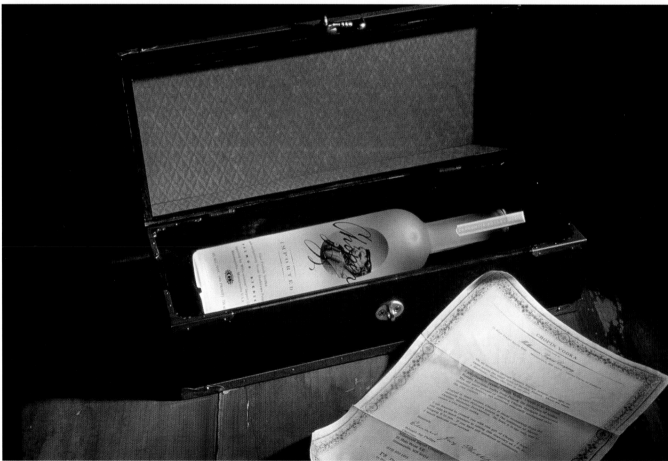

(opposite)
Design Firm: Parachute, Inc.
Creative Director: Jac Coverdale
Art Director, Designer: Heather Cooley
Photographer: Curtis Johnson
Illustrator: Mark Weakley
Copywriter: Michael Atkinson
Client: Millennium Import Co.

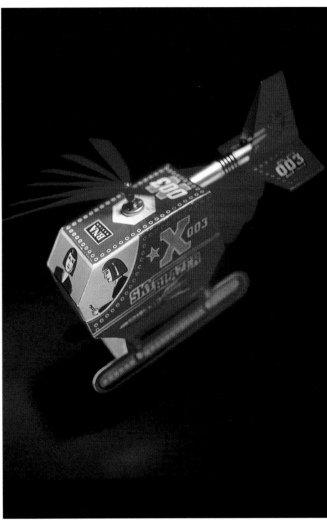

Design Firm: BNA Design Ltd. (in-house)
Creative Director: Grenville Main
Art Director: Andrew Sparrow
Designers: Sara Bellamy, Andrew Sparrow
Illustrators: Sara Bellamy,
Andrew Sparrow, Bernadette Grumbau
Client: BNA Design Ltd.

(opposite, top)
Design Firm: NB: Studio
Designers: Ben Stott, Nick Finney
Client: Knoll International

(opposite, bottom)
Design Firm: Sandstrom Design
Creative Director: Steve Sandstrom
Art Director, Designer: Jon Olsen
Client: ESPN

Design Firm: Carmichael Lynch Thorburn
Creative Director: Bill Thorburn
Designer: Chad Hagen
Photographer: Bill Phelps
Copywriter: Jonathan Sunshine
Client: Association
of Children's Health Care

Design Firm: John Brady
Design Consultants (in-house)
Art Director: John Brady
Designers: Jim Bolander, Jeff Beavers
Production: Julie Poski Lackman,
Stan Orzechowski
Design Firm: John Brady
Design Consultants

(opposite)
Design Firm: Björkman & Mitchell AB
Designer: Klas Björkman
Photographer: Ulf Dänbro
Copywriter: Helena Mohlin
Client: Ljundbergs Tryckeri Printing

Fyra
aspekter på
kvalitet

Fyra
aspekter på
kvalitet

(this page left)
Design Firm: Mires Design (in-house)
Art Director: Jose Serrano
Designers: Jose Serrano, Jeff Samaripa
Client: Mires Design

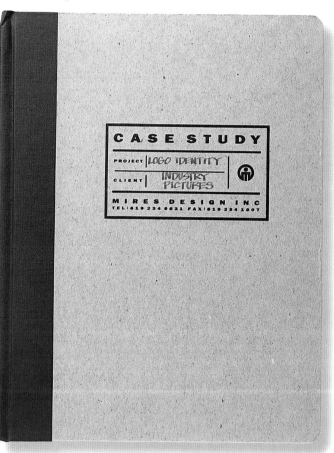

(this page right and opposite)
Design Firm: Richard Blackman Design
Creative Director: Richard Blackman
Art Director, Designer,
Illustrator: Kate Linton
Client: Austereo MCM Entertainment

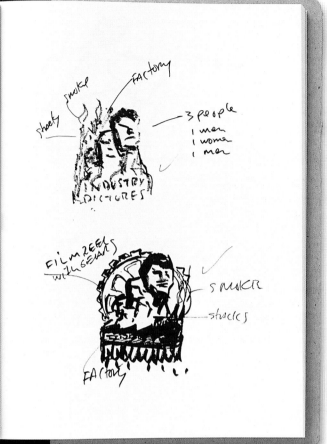

INDUSTRY PICTURES
commercial film production company

(opposite)
Design Firm: Garage Graphics
Creative Director, Art Director,
Designer: Rikard Lassenius
Photographer: Ryushi Nakagawa
Client: Nail Design

(this page)
Design Firm: Garage Graphics
Designer: Rikard Lassenius
Client: Face

Creative Director, Art Director:
Rob Hugel
Designers: Fred Decker,
Suzie Maitland-Smith
Client: Fox River Paper Company

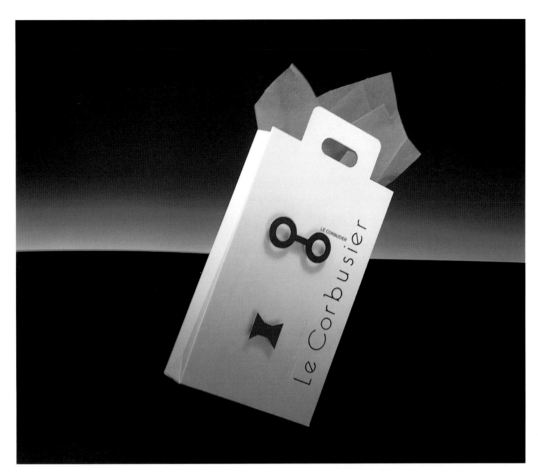

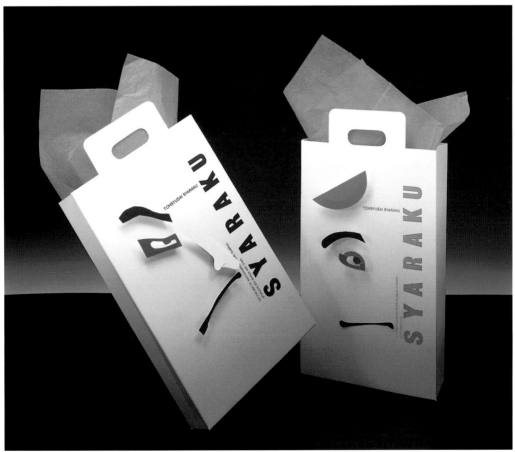

(opposite)
Design Firm: Supon Design Group
Creative Director: Supon Phornirunlit
Art Director: Maria Sese Paul
Designers: Maria Sese Paul,
Jeanette Nelson, Sharisse Steber
Client: Museum of Shoes

Design Firm: Meridian Design Studio
Art Director: Géza Sulyok
Designers: Géza Sulyok,
Zsuzsanaa Sulyok
Client: Kartonpack Printing Company

CLASSIC AMERICAN AIRCRAFT

Mustang

32 USA
1997

Model B

32 USA
1997

Cub

32 USA
1997

Vega

32 USA
1997

Alpha

32 USA
1997

B-10

32 USA
1997

Corsair

32 USA
1997

Stratojet

32 USA
1997

Gee Bee

32 USA
1997

Staggerwing

32 USA
1997

Flying Fortress

32 USA
1997

Stearman

32 USA
1997

Constellation

32 USA
1997

Lightning

32 USA
1997

Peashooter

32 USA
1997

Tri-Motor

32 USA
1997

DC-3

32 USA
1997

314 Clipper

32 USA
1997

Jenny

32 USA
1997

Wildcat

32 USA
1997

香港通用郵票
HONG KONG DEFINITIVE STAMPS

設計：靳埭強 DESIGNED BY KAN TAI-KEUNG

香港 $10   香港 $20   香港 $50

HONG KONG   HONG KONG   HONG KONG

(opposite, top)
Design Firm: Kan & Lau
Design Consultants
Creative Director, Art Director,
Designer, Photographer:
Kan Tai-Keung
Computer Illustrator: Benson
Kwun Tin Yau
Client: General Post Office

(opposite, bottom)
Design Firm:
Asprey Di Donato Design Pty. Ltd.
Client: Australia Post

(opposite)
Art Director: Michelle Watson
Illustrator: Ingo Fast
Client: Friends of Animals

(this page)
Design Firm: Mires Design
Art Director: Jose Serrano
Designers: Jose Serrano, Miguel Perez
Illustrator: Dan Thoner
Client: Hell Racer

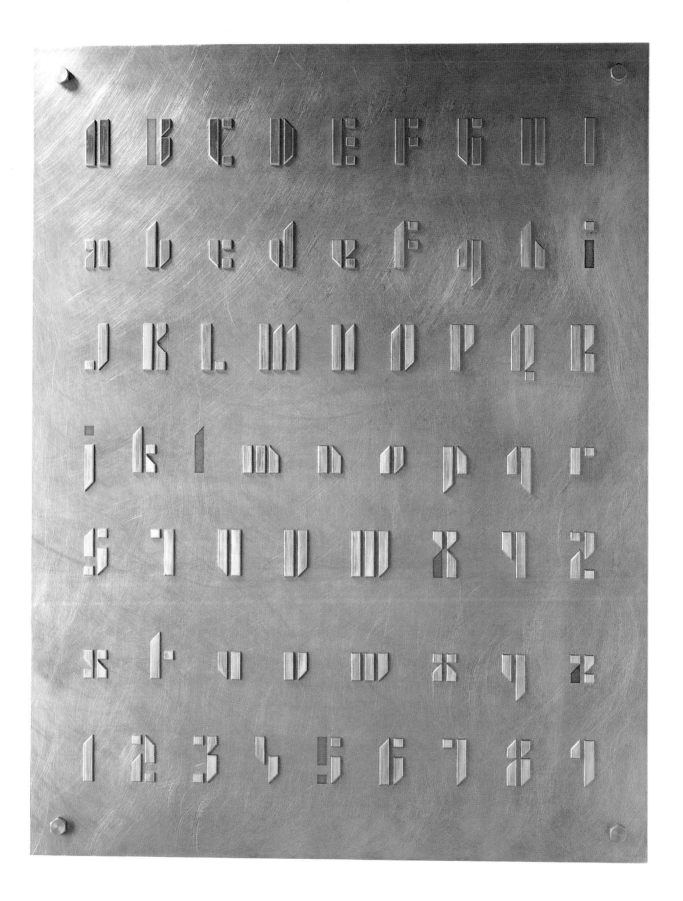

Design Firm: Alternativ Studio (in-house)
Art Director, Designer: Peter Vajda
Client: Alternativ Studio

Indices Verzeichnis Index

Creative Directors Art Directors Designers

Photographers Illustrators

Copywriters

Clients

Graphis Books Promotion

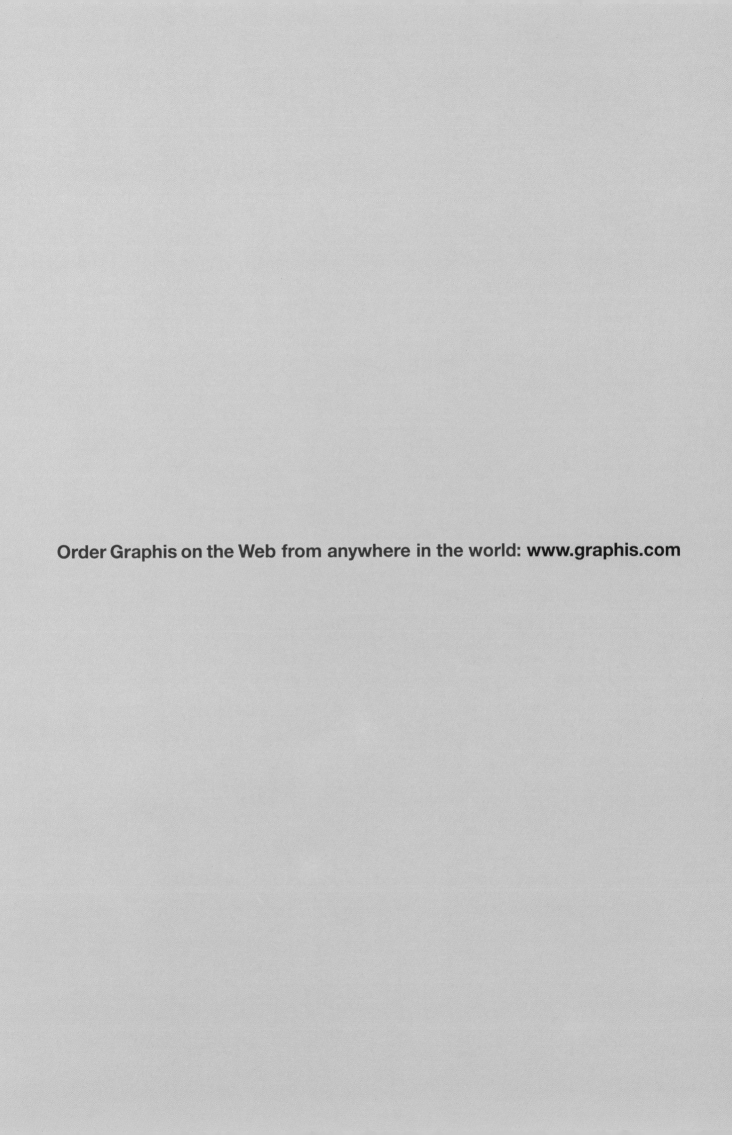

Order Graphis on the Web from anywhere in the world: www.graphis.com

Subscribe to our
Magazine and save
40% on all Books!

PosterAnnual 1998

Corporate Identity 3

Book Design 2

New Talent Design Annual 1998

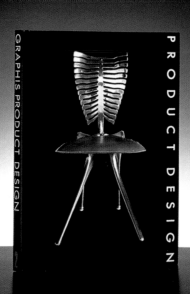

GRAPHIS PRODUCT DESIGN

PRODUCT DESIGN

T-shirtDesign 2

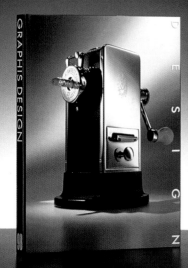

GRAPHIS DESIGN

DESIGN

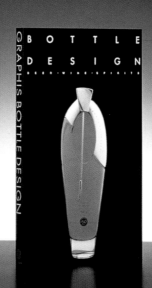

GRAPHIS BOTTLE DESIGN

BOTTLE DESIGN

AppleDesign

Order Form

As a subscriber to the magazine, you automatically qualify for a *40 percent discount* on any of our books. If you place a standing order you will receive a *50 percent discount*. This means any Graphis book you select is sent to you as soon as it comes off press, and you will be billed at half the cover price plus shipping. With a *standing order* Graphis doesn't have to go through the expense of contacting you by mail and can therefore pass the savings directly back to you. Our annuals such as Poster, Photo, Design, and Advertising come out every year. The rest of our books come out every 2-4 years. If you don't wish to receive a particular book automatically when it happens to come out just choose the *40 percent off price*. If you are not a subscriber, then you still receive a *20 percent discount*. For your support we now cover all the communication disciplines and if there is a Graphis book you care to have that is not listed, please call us and we will do everything we can to get it for you. We thank you for your support.

Book Title	Retail	Non Subscriber 20% off	Subscriber 40% off	Standing Order 50% off	Quantity	Totals	Book Title	Retail	Non Subscriber 20% off	Subscriber 40% off	Standing Order 50% off	Quantity	Totals
Spring Books 1998							**General Interest**						
Book Design 2	☐ $70	☐ $56	☐ $42	☐ $35			**Nudes 1**	☐ $40	☐ $32	☐ $24	☐ $20		
Corporate Identity 3	☐ $70	☐ $56	☐ $42	☐ $35			**Nudes 2**	☐ $50	☐ $40	☐ $30	☐ $25		
New Talent 1998	☐ $60	☐ $48	☐ $36	☐ $30			**Passion & Line**	☐ $50	☐ $40	☐ $30	☐ $25		
Poster Annual 1998	☐ $70	☐ $56	☐ $42	☐ $35			**Pool Light**	☐ $70	☐ $56	☐ $42	☐ $35		
T-Shirt 2	☐ $60	☐ $48	☐ $36	☐ $30			**Typography 2**	☐ $70	☐ $56	☐ $42	☐ $35		
Fall Books 1998							**Walter Iooss**	☐ $70	☐ $56	☐ $42	☐ $35		
Advertising 1999	☐ $70	☐ $56	☐ $42	☐ $35			**Design Books**						
Annual Reports 6	☐ $70	☐ $56	☐ $42	☐ $35			**Apple Design**	☐ $45	☐ $36	☐ $27	☐ $23		
Brochures 3	☐ $70	☐ $56	☐ $42	☐ $35			**Bottle Design**	☐ $40	☐ $32	☐ $24	☐ $20		
Design Annual 1999	☐ $70	☐ $56	☐ $42	☐ $35			**Magazine Design**	☐ $70	☐ $56	☐ $42	☐ $35		
Digital Photo 1	☐ $70	☐ $56	☐ $42	☐ $35			**Products by Design 1**	☐ $70	☐ $56	☐ $42	☐ $35		
Letterhead 4	☐ $70	☐ $56	☐ $42	☐ $35			**Products by Design 2**	☐ $70	☐ $56	☐ $42	☐ $35		
Logo Design 4	☐ $60	☐ $48	☐ $36	☐ $30			**Web Design Now**	☐ $70	☐ $56	☐ $42	☐ $35		
Photo Annual 1998	☐ $70	☐ $56	☐ $42	☐ $35									

Shipping & handling per book, US $ 5.00, Canada $ 10.00, Elsewhere $15.00		
New York State shipments add 8.25% tax		
☐ I am not a subscriber, but I want to qualify for the 20% off discount.		

Graphis Magazine	USA (shipping included)	Canada (shipping included)	Interational (shipping included)	Interational (airmail surcharge included)
One year subscription, 6 Issues	☐ $90	☐ $100	☐ $125	☐ $184
Two year subscription, 12 Issues	☐ $165	☐ $185	☐ $235	☐ $294
Student subscription, 6 Issues	☐ $59	☐ $59	☐ $80	☐ $139

☐ I am presently a Graphis magazine subscriber and therefore, qualify for the 40% discount.

Total

Name	☐ American Express ☐ Visa ☐ Mastercard ☐ Check
Company	
Address	Card #
City State Zip	Expiration
Daytime phone	Card holder's signature

Copy or send this order form and make check payable to Graphis Inc. For even faster turn-around service, or if you have any questions about subscribing call us at the following numbers in the **US (800) 209. 4234, outside the US (212) 532. 9387 ext. 242 or 241, Fax (212) 696. 4242. Graphis 141 Lexington Avenue New York, New York 10016-8193. Order Graphis on the Web from anywhere in the world: www.graphis.com**

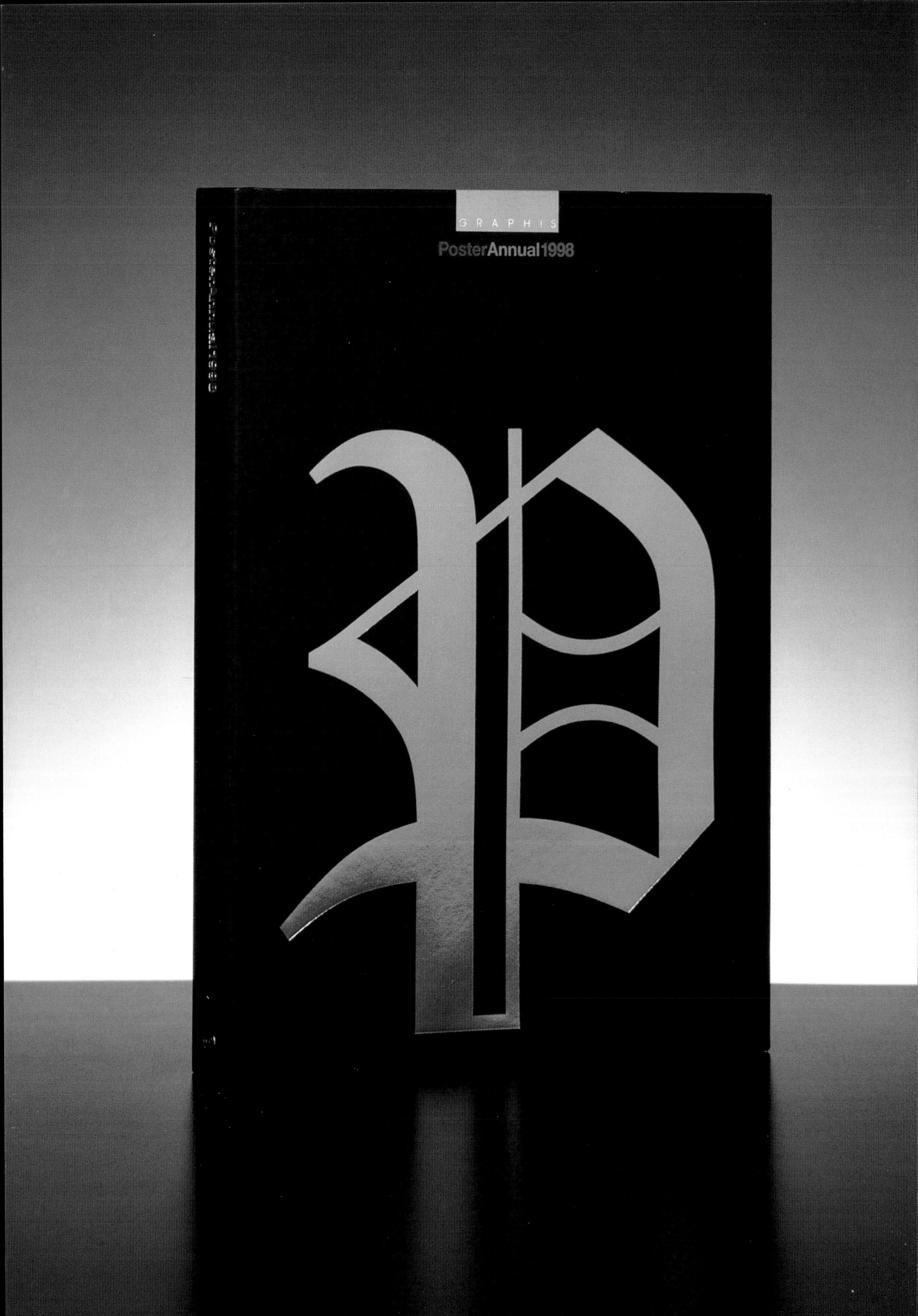

Graphis Books Call For Entry

If you would like us to put you on our mailing lists for Call for Entries for any of our books, please fill out the form and check off the specific books you would like to be a part of. We are now consolidating our mailings twice a year for our spring and fall books. If information is needed on specific deadlines for any of our books, please consult our web site: www.graphis.com.

Graphic Design Books	☐ Poster Annual	**Photography Books**	**Student Books**
☐ Advertising Annual	☐ Products by Design	☐ Digital Photo (Professional)	☐ Advertising Annual
☐ Annual Reports	☐ Letterhead	☐ Human Con. (Photojournalism)	☐ Design Annual
☐ Book Design	☐ Logo Design	☐ New Talent (Amateur)	☐ Photo Annual (Professional)
☐ Brochure	☐ Music CD	☐ Nudes (Professional)	☐ Products by Design
☐ Corporate Identity	☐ New Media	☐ Nudes (Fine Art)	☐ **All the Books**
☐ Design Annual	☐ Packaging	☐ Photo Annual (Professional)	☐ All Design Books only
☐ Digital Fonts	☐ Paper Promotions	☐ Photography (Fine Art)	☐ All Photo Books only
☐ Diagrams	☐ Typography		☐ All Students Books only

First Name: _____ Last Name: _____

Company: _____

Telephone: _____ Fax: _____

Mailing Address: _____ City: _____

State, Country: _____ Zip: _____

Copy or mail form to: Graphis, Call for Entries, 141 Lexington Ave., New York, New York 10016-819, USA, or fax to 212. 213.3229

ELEGANT DESIGN, ELEGANT PHOTOGRAPHS, ELEGANT PAPER

An idea. An idea in mind. In thoughts, in dreams. The blank sheet of paper provides the raw material for ideas, giving free reign to fantasy. Every book is based on an idea and the paper that it is written on. ZANDERS has the paper. Fine paper, suitable for every conceivable kind of communication. Because paper represents communication - worldwide. In 100 countries spread over five continents, people hold ZANDERS fine papers in their hands and use it day in, day out.

Wherever people appreciate style, the style that unites product and paper, people appreciate ZANDERS, on the label of a bottle of cognac, the band of a good cigar, or the pages of a design book, such as a Graphis title.

ZANDERS papers, with their uniform and identifiable brand names, are unmistakable worldwide. What makes more sense than to present an elegant product on an elegant paper? And holding this document in their hands, people feel the ZANDERS quality - the ikono paper's elegance.

"BEING ZANDERIZED": The ZANDERS style

ZANDERS Feinpapiere AG have a style of their own, developed out of tradition and aimed at products designed for a high-tech age. It's this tradition that represents quality, because ZANDERS does not think merely in terms of quantity.

Following the great tradition

In 1829, Johann Wilhelm Zanders founded a paper manufacturing company in Bergisch-Gladbach, to the east of Cologne. This company developed into today's ZANDERS Feinpapiere AG. Back then, it had an annual production of about 25 tons of natural vat paper and employed 40 workers at three vats.

Right from the time of the founding fathers, exacting standards were set in producing fine paper and passed on to later generations. In particular, the coating and finishing expertise ZANDERS has acquired over the years stands comparison with the best in the world. And to this day, ZANDERS has the greatest technical and aesthetic demands for paper - *the* communication vehicle.

Innovative technology: The basis of paper-making

ZANDERS has two locations in Germany. About 2,800 employees produce approximately 380,000 tons of fine paper at the Gohrsmühle and Reflex works. Here, ZANDERS' flexible equipment is designed to meet customer demands: 9 paper machines and 13 coating machines. And because innovative technology cannot be bought ready made, this equipment was specially developed in ZANDERS' own development laboratories to process ZANDERS fine papers.

The art of paper-making is based on high-quality raw materials, bought on the international markets; for example, woodpulp derived from sustainable forest management. There are also comprehensive quality controls, and the employees who make production systems work efficiently. Of course, there is also the unique ZANDERS expertise in finishing and coating. What's more, manufacturing processes at ZANDERS are certified in accordance with DIN ISO 9001.

ZANDERS has opened the way for the development of a sound and dynamic company by embarking on a restructuring process. The company will thus ensure its success well into the next millennium by manufacturing efficient products that secure specialized markets. The combination of tradition and innovation allows ZANDERS to grow purposefully in the world's markets.

The same premium quality that ZANDERS guarantees for its papers also applies to the service that it provides.

By setting up workshops for customers, ZANDERS integrates them into the development of new products and into the concept of the extended service system.

Up-to-date information, immediate feedback, as well as new communication systems such as e-mail, the Internet, and Lotus, provide additional assistance in creating a customer-friendly dialogue.

All this represents a shift in attitudes, placing the customer at the center of attention. Those who want to move companies have to move people first. And ZANDERS is moving fast.

The enormous solidarity and extraordinary commitment on the part of our employees as well as the close and trusting cooperation between ZANDERS and its partners are not the only factors that make the company so competitive in the modern market. In the last analysis, the high quality of our employees and of our work processes are what determine the quality of our products.

"We answer to the world": ZANDERS in the International Paper Group of Companies

International Paper has been the major shareholder in ZANDERS Feinpapiere AG since 1989, and it too can look back on a history that is now exactly 100 years old.

Founded in 1898 as the result of a merger of 17 paper factories in the state of New York, over the century, the company has become the largest paper and wood producer in the world. Nevertheless, the guiding principle of the founding years remains as true as ever today: keep in close contact with the customer.

Today, there are more than 80,000 employees working for the company in 31 countries, making products for clients in more than 130 nations around the world. The former paper manufacturer has long since become a diversified company. The company divisions today include packaging and wood products, and the Special Products

Division provides minerals for the automotive industry. On Wall Street in New York, International Paper is one of the 30 companies that make up the daily Dow Jones index.

Paper products: Who hasn't heard of ikono?

Many of the high-quality products that ZANDERS manufactures have now become generic terms in the marketplace: for example, CHROMOLUX. The letterhead used by the Vatican is a fine paper manufactured by ZANDERS. This writing paper with the Gohrsmühle watermark can be found on many desks.

It is not only in the world of design that ikono has become a byword for quality and functionality. ZANDERS supplies brands that are internationally known and used. At the same time, Zanders is committed to making the innovations needed for the coming age. Genuine brands are international brands.

So as to provide the company with the systematic orientation to markets and customers, ZANDERS comprises five divisions: two-sided coated papers, CHROMOLUX, ZANDERS autocopy, the special papers of International Paper Premium Papers, and ZANDERS Digital Imaging Papers.

Two-sided coated papers and boards: ZANDERS Mega & ikono

ZANDERS has more than 100 years of experience in manufacturing coated papers.

ZANDERS' division for two-sided coated paper supplies the Mega and ikono production lines. ikono is also the basis for the quality-printing of Graphis.

Cast-coated papers and boards: Chromolux

CHROMOLUX: these are cast-coated papers and boards manufactured by ZANDERS. Exactly 40 years ago ZANDERS brought one of its most convincing innovations to the market—CHROMOLUX.

To this day, CHROMOLUX stands for a unique, full range of top-quality papers and boards, coated on one or two sides, white or colored, embossed, aluminized, with mother of pearl or metallic effect, or with colored reverse.

Self-copying paper: ZANDERS Autocopy

As a leading manufacturer in the field, ZANDERS is one of the tenth largest, globally operating companies which supplies the annual total requirement of 2.5 million tons of self-copying paper.

Graphic special papers: International Paper Premium Papers

ZANDERS markets graphic special papers within the framework of a newly founded European group, "International Paper Premium Papers EWIV." "ZANDERS DEZIGN COLLECTION" is the overall brand name under which these products are presented.

ZANDERS launched an innovation offensive at the beginning of 1998 when it brought out a medley under this overall brand. Representing a completely new concept in paper, it makes possible the combination of white or cream paper with different qualities. It

caught the eyes of designers in the spring of 1998 with its off-beat appearance. After all, only paper makes ideas visible.

Product line with a future: ZANDERS imaging

The ZANDERS Imaging product line includes four brands: ZANDERS imaging digital for digital printing machines, ZANDERS imaging copy for full-colour copiers and full-colour bubble-jet printers, as well as ZANDERS Imaging jet and ZANDERS Imaging jet Pro for all kinds of high-quality applications on ink-jet printers - including photographic and poster print-outs.

Paper for a new era: ikono progress - premium paper for art prints

The world of fine papers is the world of ZANDERS. Graphis prints on the art paper for the 21st century: ikono.

The ikono product line forms part of the division for two-sided coated papers which makes up more than 50% of sales. Ikono international enjoys international recognition for its use of high-quality printed matter: business cards, calendars, art books and picture books as well as brochures and leaflets.

Ikono is an art paper. What makes it unusual is that it is a premium paper among wood-free coated papers that appeals with its outstanding print processing characteristics and excellent image quality. To name a few, special features of ikono are the unique gloss and consistency of its surface.

The two products, ikono silk and silk ivory, are specialities in the world of mattpapers. These exhibit an unusually high degree of resistance to abrasion. Ikono gloss, matt, and color (seven colors), complete the range of paper qualities.

Many years of experience combined with flexible and efficient production facilities and a comprehensive range of stocks, enable the supply of special requirements in terms of format and basis weight as well as particular surface embossing.

The ikono range has been optimized and extended enough to confirm its position as a premium paper for the 21st century. Anyone who wants to demonstrate the highest quality of products, companies, or print media is sure to want to use ZANDERS ikono.

Ikono - simply the best.

ZANDERS completes the cycle: Idea-paper-printing

ZANDERS makes use of its marketing organization by trading in a global network. As a manufacturer of fine paper, it makes its papers available to its customers at the same quality anywhere in the world. Exports always have an important role in the paper industry - and this applies to ZANDERS too.

ZANDERS Contacts: If you want to know more

Information on ZANDERS products and marketing partners may be obtained via the following marketing companies or directly from the Zanders head offices in Germany.

Die Idee. Die Idee sitzt im Kopf, in den Gedanken, in den Träumen. Das leere Blatt Papier. Spielraum der Phantasie und Rohstoff für Ideen zugleich. Mit der Idee und dem Papier beginnt jedes Buch. ZANDERS hat das Papier. Feinpapier, geeignet für alle nur erdenklichen Arten der Kommunikation. Denn Papier ist Kommunikation. Weltweit.

In 100 Ländern auf fünf Kontinenten halten Menschen ZANDERS Feinpapiere in den Händen und nutzen es tagtäglich. Überall wo Menschen Stil schätzen, und Stil Produkt und Papier verbindet. Das Etikett der Cognac Flasche, die Banderole einer guten Zigarre oder die Seiten eines Design-Buchs. Wie Graphis! ZANDERS Papiere sind unverwechselbar. Sie werden weltweit unter ihrem einheitlichen und identifizierenden Markennamen angeboten. Was liegt näher, als ein edles Produkt auf edlem Papier zu präsentieren? Halten Menschen diese Graphis–Dokumentation in der Hand, spüren Sie ZANDERS-Qualität - das Papier ikono.

„BEING ZANDERIZED": Der ZANDERS Stil

Das „Z" hat für ZANDERS eine besondere Bedeutung. Im Zeichen des „Z" setzt die ZANDERS Feinpapiere AG die zielgerichtete Entwicklung von Produkten für das High–Tech–Zeitalter fort. Und es ist vor allem ein Qualitätssiegel eines deutschen Traditions-herstellers. Denn bei ZANDERS wird nicht nur in „Tonnen" gedacht.

Der Tradition verpflichtet

1829 gründete Johann Wilhelm Zanders in Bergisch Gladbach, östlich von Köln, jenes Unternehmen der Papierherstellung, das sich zur heutigen ZANDERS Feinpapiere AG entwickelt hat. Die Jahresproduktion lag zu dieser Zeit bei etwa 25 Tonnen Natur-Büttenpapier. Es gab 40 Mitarbeiter, die an drei Bütten arbeiteten. Schon die Gründerväter haben hohe Qualitätsansprüche an das Produkt Feinpapier gestellt und ihre Erfahrungen über Generationen weitergegeben. Vor allem das über Jahre erworbene Streich- und Veredelungs-Kow-how ist im weltweiten Vergleich erstklassig. Bis heute stellt ZANDERS höchste technische und ästhetische Ansprüche an den Kommunikationsträger Papier.

Innovative Technologie als Stützen der weißen Kunst

ZANDERS ist an zwei Standorten in Deutschland vertreten. In den Werken Gohrsmühle und Reflex produzieren rund 2.800 Mitarbeiter etwa 380.000 Tonnen Feinpapier. Dort steht das flexible und auf die Ansprüche der Kunden konzipierte Equipment: 9 Papier- und 13 Streichmaschinen. Sie verarbeiten ZANDERS Feinpapiere, entwickelt in eigenen Forschungslaboren, denn innovative Technologie gibt es nicht von der Stange.

Hochwertige Rohstoffe, auf den internationalen Märkten eingekauft, zum Beispiel Zellstoffe aus nachhaltiger Forstwirtschaft, umfassende Qualitätskontrollen, Mitarbeiter, die Produktionsanlagen effizient machen - das sind die Eckpfeiler der weißen Kunst - der Papierherstellung. Und natürlich das einzigartige ZANDERS Know how in der Veredelung und beim Streichen. Übrigens: Die Produktions-abläufe bei ZANDERS sind nach der DIN ISO 9001 zertifiziert.

Mit einem Umstrukturierungsprozeß hat ZANDERS den Weg für ein schlagkräftiges und solides Unternehmen freigemacht. Ein Unternehmen, das auch im nächsten Jahrtausend nachhaltig Erfolg haben und mit leistungsfähigen Produkten spezialisierte Märkte gewinnen wird. Ein agiler Innovator mit Tradition wächst zielstrebig in die Märkte der Welt. Dieselbe Premium-Qualität, die ZANDERS für seine Papiere garantiert, soll auch für den Service gelten.

ZANDERS bindet Kunden in Rahmen von Workshops in die Entwicklung neuer Produkte und in die Konzeption erweiternder Servicesysteme ein. Aktuelle Informationen, sofortiges Feed Back-neue Kommunikationssysteme wie e-mail, Internet, Lotus helfen beim kundennahen Dialog. Die Wende vom „Ich" zum „Sie" hat begonnen. Wer Unternehmen bewegen will, muß Menschen bewegen. Und ZANDERS ist in Bewegung.

Ein erstarkendes Zusammengehörigkeitsgefühl und das außergewöhnliche Engagement der Mitarbeiter sowie die enge, vertrauensvolle Zusammenarbeit zwischen Marktpartnern und ZANDERS zeichnen nicht zuletzt die Konkurrenzfähigkeit des Unternehmens aus. Denn die Qualität der Mitarbeiter und der Arbeitsprozesse sind nicht zuletzt die Qualität eines Produktes.

„WE ANSWER TO THE WORLD":

ZANDERS im Unternehmensverbund von International Paper

Seit 1989 ist International Paper Mehrheitsaktionär bei der ZANDERS Feinpapiere AG und kann ebenfalls auf eine jetzt genau 100 jährige Geschichte zurückblicken.

1898 als Zusammenschluß von 17 Papierfabriken im US-Bundesstaat New York gegründet, stieg das Unternehmen im Laufe eines Jahrhunderts zum größten Papier- und Holzhersteller der Welt auf. Trotzdem zählt auch heute noch der Grundsatz, der bereits in den Jahren der Gründung die oberste Maxime war: Eng

Werk Gohrsmühle, Papiermaschine 3

mit den Kunden zusammenarbeiten.

Heute gehören dern Unternehmen über 80.000 Mitarbeiter an, die in 31 Ländern für Auftraggeber in mehr als 130 Staaten der Welt Produkte fertigen. Längst ist aus dem einstigen Papierhersteller ein diversifiziertes Unternehmen geworden. Zu den Unternehmensbereichen zählen heute auch Verpackungen und Holzprodukte, genau wie im Bereich Spezialprodukte Mineralien für die Automobilindustrie. An der New Yorker Wall Street gehört International Paper zu den 30 Unternehmen, nach denen täglich der Dow-Jones-Index berechnet wird.

Produkte der weißen Kunst. Wer Kennt nicht ikono?

Viele der hochwertigen Produktnamen des Unternehmens ZANDERS sind mittlerweile zum Gattungsbegriff geworden, zum Beispiel CHROMOLUX. Die Briefbogen des Vatikan sind Feinpapiere von ZANDERS. Ikono ist nicht nur in der Welt des Designs zum Synonym für Qualität und Funktionalität geworden. Auf vielen Schreibtischen liegt Briefpapier mit dem Wasserzeichen der Gohrsmühle.

ZANDERS bietet Marken, international bekannt und angewandt. Und engagiert sich im selben Augenblick für Innovationen einer kommenden Epoche. Echte Marken besitzen Internationalität.

In Hinblick auf eine konsequente Markt- und Kundernorientierung ist das Unternehmen in fünf Sparten bzw. Bereiche gegliedert: 2seitig gestrichene Papiere, CHROMOLUX, ZANDERS autocopy, den Spezialpapieren von International Paper Premium Papers und ZANDERS Digital Imaging Papers.

2seitig gestrichene Papiere und Kartons: ZANDERS Mega & ikono

Über eine mehr als hundertjährige Erfahrung verfügt ZANDERS in der Herstellung gestrichener Papiere.

In der Sparte der 2seitig gestrichenen Papiere bietet ZANDERS die Produktlinien ZANDERS Mega und ikono an. ikono-Qualität ist auch die Grundlage für den Druck von Graphis.

Gußgestrichene Papiere und Kartons: Chromolux

CHROMOLUX - das sind gußgestrichene Papiere und Kartons von ZANDERS. Genau 40 Jahre ist es her, daß ZANDERS eine ihrer überzeugendsten innovationen auf den Mark brachte - und damit innerhalb kürzester Zeit einen Gattungsbegriff prägte: CHROMOLUX. Dieser Name steht bis heute für ein einzigartiges Vollsortiment aus Spitzenpapieren- und kartons, ein- oder beidseitig gestrichen, weiß oder farbig, geprägt, aluminiumbedampft, mit Perlmutt - oder Metalliceffekt oder farbiger Rückseite. Im Vordergrund stehen Farben, die das Design und Marketing der kommenden Jahre prägen werden und eng mit den Grundstimmungen der Jahrtsausendwende als Beginn einer neuen Epoche, verbunden sind.

Das selbstdurchschreibende Papier: ZANDERS autocopy

ZANDERS gehört als einer der führenden Hersteller zu den zehn größten, weltweit operierenden Unternehmen, die den jährlichen Gesamtbedarf von 2,5 Mio. Tonnen selbstdurchschreibender Papiere abdecken.

Graphische Spezialpapiere: International Paper Premium Papers

Graphische Spezialpapiere vermarktet ZANDERS innerhalb einer neugegründeten europäischen Gesellschaft „International Paper Premium Papers EWIV." Diese Produkte werden unter der Dachmarke „ZANDERS Dezign Collection" präsentiert.

Mit der Innovationsoffensive zu Beginn des Jahres 1998 brachte ZANDERS unter dieser Dachmarke medley hervor. Ein völlig neues Papierkonzept, das die Kombination von weißem oder cremefarbenen Papier unterschiedliche Papiercharakteristika möglich macht. Mit einem ungewöhnlichen Auftritt, in Hinblick auf Werbung und Papiermuster, hat ZANDERS das Produkt im Frühjahr 1998 an den Arbeitsplatz des Designers gebracht. Denn erst Papier macht Ideen sichtbar.

Produktlinie mit Zukunft: ZANDERS Imaging

Die Produktlinie ZANDERS Imaging zählt vier Marken: ZANDERS Imaging digital für Digitaldruckmaschinen, ZANDERS Imaging copy für Vollfarbkopierer und Vollfarblaserdrucker sowie ZANDERS Imaging jet und ZANDERS Imaging jet Pro für alle Arten von hochwertigen Anwendungen auf Tintenstrahldruckern - bis hin zum Foto- und Posterausdrucken.

Papier einer neuen Epoche: Ikono Progress Premiumpapier des Kunstdrucks

Die Welt der Feinpapiere ist die Welt von ZANDERS. Graphis ist gedruckt auf den Kunstdruckpapier für das 21. Jahrhundert: ikono.

Die Produktlinie ikono gehört zu der Sparte 2seitig gestrichene Papiere, die mit über 50 Prozent am Absatz beteiligt ist. Einsatz und Anerkennung findet ikono international im Bereich hochwertiger Druckobjekte: Geschäftsberichte, Kalender, Kunstbücher und Bildbände sowie Broschüren und Prospekte.

ikono ist ein Kunstdruckpapier. Das Besondere: Mit ikono wird das Premiumpapier im Segment der holzfrei gestrichenen Papiere angeboten, das durch seine hervorragenden drucktechnischen Verarbeitungseigenschaften und seine ausgezeichnete Bildqualität überzeugt. Besondere Merkmale von ikono sind die einzigartige Glätte und Geschlossenheit der Papieroberfläche.

Eine Spezialität in der Welt der Mattpapiere stellen die Produkte ikono silk und silk elfenbein dar, die sich durch eine ungewöhnliche Scheuerfestigkeit auszeichnen. ikono gloss, matt und color, das in sieben Farben angeboten wird, vervollständigen das Spektrum der Papierqualitäten.

Langjährige Erfahrung kombiniert mit flexiblen und leistungsfähigen Produktionsanlagen und einem umfassenden Lagerprogramm machen Sonderwünsche bei Format und Flächengewicht sowie besondere Oberflächenprägungen möglich.

Durch Produktoptimierung und Erweiterung des Einsatzspektrums bestätigt das ikono-Programm seine Position als Premium-Papier für das 21. Jahrhundert.

Wer Höchste Qualität von Produkten, Unternehmen oder Printmedien zeigen will, kommt an ZANDERS ikono nicht vorbei. ikono - simply the best.

ZANDERS-Kontakt: Wenn Sie mehr wissen wollen

Der Kreis schließt sich: Idee - Papier - Druck. ZANDERS hat mit seiner Vertriebsorganisation den Handel im globalen Netz verwirklicht. Der Feinpapierhersteller kann seinen Kunden weltweit seine Papiere in gleicher Qualität zur Verfügung stellen. Der Export ist ohnehin ein wichtiger Motor der Papierkonjunktur- auch bei ZANDERS.

Informationen zu ZANDERS-Produkten und Vertriebspartnern sind über die nachstehenden Vertriebsgeseilschaften zu erhalten oder direkt in der ZANDERS Hauptverwaltung in Deutschland.

A DESIGN ET PHOTOGRAPHIES RARES, PAPIER RARE

L'idée. L'idée germe dans l'esprit, dans les pensées, dans les rîves. La feuille blanche. A la fois champ d'expression pour l'imagination et matière brute à idées. C'est sur une idée et sur le papier que naît chaque livre.

Ce papier, ZANDERS l'a. Du papier surfin, convenant à tous les types de communication imaginables. Car le papier est communication. Dans le monde entier. Dans 100 pays, répartis sur les cinq continents, des gens tiennent entre leurs mains du papier surfin ZANDERS et l'emploient chaque jour.

Partout où l'on apprécie le style, et où le style résulte d'une subtile combinaison produit-papier. L'étiquette de la bouteille de cognac, la bague d'un bon cigare ou les pages d'un livre de design. De véritables prouesses graphiques!

Impossible de confondre les papiers ZANDERS. Partout, ils sont proposés sous un même nom, unique et reconnu. Présenter un produit rare sur un papier rare, y a-t-il démarche plus naturelle? Quiconque tient entre ses mains une telle réalisation graphique perçoit la qualité ZANDERS - le papier Medley.

„BEING ZANDERIZED": Le style ZANDERS

Pour ZANDERS, le „Z" a une signification particulière. Sous le signe du „Z", Zanders Feinpapiere AG poursuit avec zéle le développement de produits destinés à l'ère high-tech.

Mais il s'agit avant tout du label de qualité d'un fabricant allemand traditionnel. Car chez ZANDERS, on ne pense pas seulement „volume."

Tradition oblige

C'est en 1829 que Johann Wilhelm Zanders créait à Bergisch Galdbach, à l'est de Cologne, sa papeterie, devenue aujourd'hui la ZANDERS Feinpapiere AG. La production annuelle atteignait à l'époque environ 25 tonnes de papier naturel. Les 40 employés d'alors s'affairaient autour de trois cuves.

Les pères fondateurs attachaient déjà une grande importance à la qualité du produit et leur expérience s'est transmise par-delà les générations. C'est avant tout l'excellence de son savoir-faire en matière de couchage et de façonnage, acquis au cours de longues années, qui distingue l'entreprise, la hissant en ce domaine au plus haut niveau mondial. ZANDERS se montre toujours aussi exigeante sur les critères techniques et esthétiques du vecteur de communication qu'est le papier.

L'innovation technologique, recette infaillible de la „magie blanche"

ZANDERS est implantée sur deux sites en Allemagne. Dans les usines Gohrsmühle et Reflex, environ 2800 salariés produisent quelque 380000 tonnes de papier surfin. Elles sont dotées d'un équipement flexible et conçu pour répondre aux exigences des clients: 9 machines à papier et 13 coucheuses. Celles-ci fabriquent le papier ZANDERS, que la firme développe dans ses propres laboratoires de recherche, car l'innovation technologique ne s'improvise pas.

Des matires premières de haute qualité, achetées sur les marchés internationaux (la cellulose, par exemple, provient d'exploitations forestières durables), des contrôles de qualité globaux, une main-d'œuvre optimisant les performances de l'outil de production - telles sont les recettes infaillibles du tour de „magie blanche" auquel on peut assimiler la fabrication du papier. Le tout complété bien sûr par le savoir-faire inimitable de ZANDERS en matière de couchage et de façonnage. Sans oublier la certification DIN ISO 9001 obtenue par l'entreprise.

Moyennant une réorganisation, ZANDERS s'est donné les moyens d'être une entreprise à la fois solide et „battante". Une entreprise qui devrait connaître un succès durable au cours du prochain millénaire et conquérir des marchés „techniques" grâce à des produits performants. Un innovateur habile, s'appuyant sur une longue tradition, assoit obstinément sa place au sein des marchés mondiaux. Cette qualité „premium", que ZANDERS garantit pour ses papiers, doit aussi s'appliquer aux services. ZANDERS réunit ses clients dans le cadre de rencontres-qualité permettant la mise au point de nouveaux produits et la conception de formules de services élargies.

Des informations à jour, un feed-back immédiat et l'emploi de nouveaux systèmes de communication, tels que l'e-mail, Internet et Lotus, contribuent à un dialogue avec le client, avant tout basé sur l'écoute. Le passage du „nous" au „vous" a commencé.

Pour dynamiser une entreprise, il faut dynamiser les hommes. Et ZANDERS est dynamique.

Une forte solidarité et l'engagement extraordinaire des collaborateurs, de même que l'étroite relation de confiance que ZANDERS entretient avec ses partenaires commerciaux, voilà ce qui fait avant tout la compétitivité de l'entreprise. Car la qualité d'un produit ne va pas sans celle des collaborateurs et des processus.

„WE ANSWER TO THE WORLD": ZANDERS dans le groupe „International Paper"

Depuis 1989, International Paper - qui peut également se prévaloir d'un siècle d'histoire - est actionnaire majoritaire de la ZANDERS Feinpapiere AG.

Fondée en 1898 suite au regroupement de 17 papeteries de l'état de New-York aux Etats-Unis, l'entreprise est devenue en l'espace d'un siècle le plus gros producteur mondial de papier et de bois. Malgré cela, le principe directeur (= collaborer étroitement avec le client), qui constituait déjà la maxime suprême au temps où fut fondée la société, n'a rien perdu de son actualité.

Aujourd'hui, l'entreprise regroupe plus de 80000 collaborateurs qui, dans 31 pays, fabriquent des produits destinés à des donneurs d'ordre répartis dans plus de 130 nations. Il y a longtemps que l'ancien fabricant de papier a entamé sa diversification. De nos jours, l'entreprise opère également dans les secteurs de l'emballage et des produits du bois, ainsi que dans celui des minéraux spéciaux destinés à l'industrie automobile. A Wall Street, International Paper fait partie des 30 entreprises entrant quotidiennement dans le calcul de l'indice Dow-Jones.

Les produits de la „magie blanche": Qui ne connaît pas ikono?

De nombreuses appellations de produits haut de gamme, créées par la société ZANDERS, sont entre-temps devenues des notions génériques, comme CHROMOLUX. Les papiers à en-tête du Vatican sont des papiers ZANDERS. Sur d'innombrables bureaux, on trouve le papier à filigrane Gohrsmühle. Il n'y a pas que dans le monde du design qu'ikono est devenu synonyme de qualité et de fonctionnalité.

ZANDERS propose des marques connues et utilisées dans le monde entier. Dans le même temps, elle s'engage dans l'innovation afin de satisfaire les besoins à venir.

Les vraies marques possèdent une internationalité.

Pour rendre plus cohérente son orientation marché / client, l'entreprise a été divisée en cinq secteurs / domaines: papier couché 2 faces, „CHROMOLUX", ZANDERS „autocopy", les papiers spéciaux d'International Paper „Premium Papers" et ZANDERS „Digital Imaging Papers".

Papiers et cartons couchés deux faces: ZANDERS Mega & ikono

ZANDERS s'appuie sur une expérience de plus d'un siècle dans la fabrication de papiers couchés.

Dans le domaine des papiers couchés deux faces, ZANDERS propose les lignes de produits Mega et ikono. La qualité ikono constitue Également la référence de base pour l'impression graphique.

Papiers et cartons couchés haute brillance: Chromolux

Chromolux - ce sont les papiers et cartons couchés haute brillance de ZANDERS.

Il y a exactement 40 ans, ZANDERS mettait sur le marché l'une de ses innovations les plus réussies - et forgeait du même coup, en un temps très court, une notion générique: le CHROMOLUX.

Ce nom est aujourd'hui synonyme d'une gamme complète et unique de papiers haut de gamme et de cartons couchés une ou deux faces, blancs ou colorés, gaufrés, aluminisés, avec effet nacré ou métallique ou verso coloré. En vedette: les couleurs qui marqueront le design et le marketing des prochaines années et qui sont étroitement liées aux tendances de fond de cette fin de siècle, avènement d'une nouvelle époque.

Le papier autocopiant: ZANDERS autocopy

ZANDERS compte parmi les dix principaux fabricants mondiaux de papiers autocopiants, dont la consommation annuelle mondiale est de 2,5 millions de tonnes.

Papiers spéciaux arts graphiques: International Paper Premium Papers

ZANDERS commercialise des papiers spéciaux arts graphiques au sein du GIE européen „International Paper Premium Papers EWIV", récemment fondé. Ces produits sont présentés sous la marque commune „ZANDERS Dezign Colection".

Avec l'offensive menée début 1998, ZANDERS a mis en vedette, sous cette marque générique, „medley". Un tout nouveau concept permettant de marier des papiers blancs ou crème aux propriétés différentes. Grâce à une mise en scène insolite du point de vue de la publicité et de l'échantillonnage, ZANDERS est parvenue, au printemps 1998, à faire entrer ce papier dans les bureaux des designers. Car il n'y a que sur le papier que l'idée devient visible.

Une ligne de produits d'avenir: ZANDERS Imaging

La ligne de produits ZANDERS „Imaging" compte quatre marques: ZANDERS „Imaging digital" pour les machines à impression numérique, Zanders „Imaging copy" destinée aux photocopieurs et imprimantes laser couleurs ainsi que ZANDERS „Imaging jet" et ZANDERS „Imaging jet Pro" convenant à tous types d'applications haut de gamme sur imprimantes à jet d'encre - jusqu'`à l'impression de photos et de posters.

Le papier de l'ère nouvelle: Ikono progress - papier „premium" pour impression artistique

Les papiers surfins, un monde que ZANDERS connaît bien. Les graphismes s'impriment sur ikono - le papier du 21ème siècle.

La ligne ikono fait partie de la branche „papiers couchés deux faces", qui représente plus de 50% du chiffre d'affaires. ikono est reconnu et utilisé internationalement dans le domaine de l'impression haut de gamme: rapports d'activités, calendriers, livres d'art et albums, de même que brochures et prospectus.

ikono est un papier pour l'impression artistique. Sa particularité: il permet de proposer, sur le segment des papiers couchés sans bois, un papier „premium" qui convainc par ses remarquables propriétés techniques et son excellente qualité optique, son lissé inimitable et l'homogénéité de sa surface.

Les produits „ikono silk" et „ikono silk elfenbein" (=ivoire) constituent une spécialité dans l'univers des papiers mats; ils se caractérisent par leur remarquable résistance au frottement. ikono „glass", „matt" et „color", proposé en sept coloris, parachèvent la gamme.

Une longue expérience, conjuguée à un outil de production flexible et performant et à un éventail de stocks complet permettent de répondre à tous les souhaits particuliers en termes de formats et de grammages ainsi que de gaufrages spéciaux de la surface.

Grâce à l'optimisation du produit et à l'élargissement des possibilités d'utilisation, la gamme ikono confirme sa position de papier „premium" pour le 21ème siècle.

S'agit-il de vanter la qualité de produits, d'entreprises ou de médias écrits? ZANDERS ikono est incontournable. ikono - simply the best.

Contacter ZANDERS. Si vous désirez en savoir plus:

La boucle est bouclée: Idée - Papier - Impression

Grâce à sa structure de distribution, ZANDERS a su donner corps au „commerce en réseau global". Le fabricant de papiers surfins peut mettre à la disposition de ses clients du monde entier des papiers de qualité identique. L'export continue d'ailleurs d'être un moteur conjoncturel important dans le secteur du papier - et il n'en va pas autrement chez ZANDERS.

Pour obtenir des informations sur les produits ZANDERS et les partenaires distributeurs, vous pouvez vous adresser aux sociétés de distribution suivantes ou directement au siège central de ZANDERS en Allemagne.

ZANDERS Feinpapiere AG
An der Gohrsmühle
D- 51465 Bergische Gladbach
Tel.: 02202/ 15- 0
Fax.: 02202/ 15- 2806

ZANDERS Benelux S.P.R.L.
Residentie Boudelo
Plezantstraat 43
B- 9100 St. Niklass
Belgium
Tel.: +32-3-7 65-98 69
Fax.: +32-3-7 65-98 74

ZANDERS Fine Papers Ltd.
2 Kings Hill Avenue
Kings HIll, West Malling
Kent ME 19 4AQ, Great Britain
Tel.: +44-17 32-59 1900
Fax.: +44-17 32-59 9090

ZANDERS Iberia S.L.
Joan Güell, 149, entlo. C
08028 Barcelona, Spain
Tel.: +34-3-791-4212
Fax.: +34-3-339-9550

ZANDERS Italia S.R.L.
Viale Milanofiori,
Strada 1, pal. F
1-20090 Assago (MI), Italy
Tel.: +39-0-25751-2783
Fax.: +39-0-25751-2843

ZANDERS USA, Inc.
100 Demarest Drive
Wayne, NJ 07470, USA
Tel.: +1-973-305-1990
Fax.: +1-973-305-1888

Europapier S.A.
Route de Piscop - BP 30
F-95350 Saint-Brice
sous Forét, France
Tel.: +33-1-393325-00
Fax.: +33-1-393325-42